I0016781

# NIST 800-171 rev. 1
## *Post-Secondary Education*
## *Cyber-Guidebook*

*INCLUDES: Emerging Supply Chain Risk Management (SCRM) Challenges*

**Mark A. Russo**
*Former Chief Information Security Officer (CISO), Department of Education*

Syber-Risk
.com

## DEDICATION

*This book is dedicated to the cyber-security men and women that protect and defend the Information Systems of this great Nation.*

*This is also dedicated to my family who have been supportive of my endeavors to plunge into writing as not just a hobby but a calling to make the world a better and safer place.*

**NIST 800-171 rev. 1:** *Post-Secondary Cyber-Guidebook* ~*SECOND EDITION*

by Mark A. Russo

Copyright © 2019 Syber-Risk.com LLC. All rights reserved.

Printed in the United States of America.

April 2019:        Second Edition

**Revision History for the First Edition**

2019:              First Release

# On September 1, 2018, We Launched the _Most Extensive_ Cybersecurity Blog Site

*This is the major resource of everything "Cyber."*
*"The good, the bad, and the ugly of cybersecurity all in one place."*

**Join us at** https://cybersentinel.tech

*This free resource is available to everyone interested in the fate and future of cybersecurity in the 21st Century*

# NIST 800-171 rev. 1:
## Post-Secondary Education Cyber-Guidebook

## Table of Contents

# Forward

In 2016, I walked into a serious mess at the Department of Education (ED). ED had no email encryption, Data Loss Prevention (DLP) capability, or functioning Security Operations Center (SOC). The Chief Information Officer (CIO) at the time was under investigation by the House Oversight Committee and had addressed NO cybersecurity findings for more than five years. Allegations of running a business and using employing ED employees after hours plagued ED and its soon to resign CIO. Working with a very small team and lacking any support by the new "political-hack" CIO, my team and I was able to close over 95% of the outstanding US Congressional and Inspector General cybersecurity shortfall weaknesses that had plagued a highly under resourced and understaffed Directorate at ED.

I have also updated this version with a simplified approach to addressing the growing challenges of Cybersecurity Supply Chain Risk management (Cy-SCRM). It is intended as a start point for companies, agencies, colleges, and universities to have a flowchart to start protecting their IT hardware and software buys. I truly hope this is a ground-breaking approach offered to the entire cybersecurity profession. If you have ideas, complaints, or comments you can reach me at my 2018 site, The Cyber Sentinel, https://cybersentinel.tech. I look forward to your thoughts as well as "we stop the bad guys." ™

# NIST SP 800-171 for Colleges and Universities

**I HAVE TO LAUGH.** The Deloitte's 2017 guide, *NIST Special Publication 800-171 for Higher Education*, (https://library.educause.edu/resources/2016/4/an-introduction-to-nist-special-publication-800-171-for-higher-education-institutions) it states that "traditional approaches to cybersecurity in higher education are no longer adequate," and if they are describing a move from lackluster and ad hoc patching procedures, there is still a great amount of improvement needed within the halls of colleges and universities nationally. The need to protect vital US government research from the Chinese, Russians, and Iranians has only seen small improvements in the past few years. The need and requirement to effectively, and to honestly, implement NIST 800-171 is still in its *infantile* stage.

NIST 800-171 is NOT just about the protections of Controlled Unclassified Information (CUI). It is about positive control of information to only those with the proper need to know. The Chinese People's Liberation Army (PLA) should not be able to gather information about Intellectual Property (IP) belonging to the US Government, but the US taxpayer more specifically. NIST 800-171 is that move toward real protections. This book is designed as a how-to book for cybersecurity professionals at US colleges and universities, and as needed, beyond.

This book is written as a step-by-step approach to the 110 security controls. Not all controls need to address immediately, but must be documented, monitored, and managed during the life of the system and data housed within university data centers. Additionally, included are the additional "sub-controls" that were released in June 2018. While this has added to the number of total controls, if the cybersecurity professional or specialist has completely implemented the base control, many of these added controls can be easily answered and addressed to government contract oversight officials.

There is still much more work that needs to be done in the area of cybersecurity. We are constantly reminded of ongoing intrusions to both public and private sector websites. What we do here, unlike so many books and articles, is that we describe the "how" to do and fix the specific control. While the challenges are many and everchanging, the objective of this book is to provide you an initial start-point with many directions to good and complete resources to protect not just CUI data, but the overall IP of your college, university, or research facility.

# The History of Cybersecurity-SCRM[1] (Cy-SCRM)

The history of Cy-SCRM[2] can be traced to the year 2006. Shortly after the Chinese company Lenovo purchased International Business Machine's (IBM) personal computing division, the use or purchase of Lenovo Personal Computer (PC) "...due to backdoor vulnerabilities" (Infosec Institute, 2013) was banned. A discreet ban by several Western nations, to include the US, was initiated against the Chinese firm of **Lenovo** Personal Computers. While there were no specific unclassified details of any corruption of the supply chain of malicious code it was during this time that industry and the Congress of the United States recognized the far-reaching damage China could have to the global supply chain.

In 2012, the House Permanent Select Committee on Intelligence had major concerns about the threats facing the telecommunications hardware devices and software developments from China. This included the possibility of electronic "eavesdropping" within the confines of US business and agency IT environments. Specific to its investigation of the operating practices of a Chinese IT company, Huawei Technologies, _Huawei (Wah-way) Technologies Company,_ the committee reported that: "The threat posed [by Huawei/China] to U.S. national-security interests... in the telecommunications supply chain is an increasing priority..." (US House of Representatives, 2012, p.1)--the concerns about Huawei have become even more heightened under the Trump Administration in 2018 and 2019. The fears continue to manifest as China pursues becoming an international economic superpower and a potential threat the supply chain.

In February 2015, the Director of National Intelligence (DNI), identified a major risk facing the United States (US) within the "Cyber" domain was the potential insertion of malicious code into IT hardware and software items sold to the US. The DNI, James R. Clapper, stated the following: "despite ever-improving network defenses, the diverse possibilities for...supply chain operations to insert compromised hardware or software...will hold nearly all [Information and Communication Technology] systems at risk for years to come" (DNI, 2015, p.1). It was most likely at this time that the Intelligence Community (IC) was compelled to share its concerns about a growing threat; a threat that may have been of dramatic concern especially within its own IT environments.

---

[1] While the more accurate term is Cybersecurity-SCRM (Cy-SCRM), for the purposes of this edition we will stay with the more expansive term. Expect this term to change within the next year to more accurately describe this aspect of cybersecurity protection measures and controls.

**James R. Clapper, DNI (August 15, 2010 – January 20, 2017)**

Specifically, Huawei represents a pervasive threat to the international IT supply chain. Huawei has both the means and motives to compromise IT equipment and systems on the behalf of the Chinese government. "…Huawei has refused to explain its relationship with the Chinese government or the role of the Communist Party…inside the company…" (Simonite, 2012). It may be assumed, based on multiple Huawei senior leaders having close ties with the People's Liberation Army (PLA), that Huawei has an explicit connection with the Chinese government and its strategic objectives.

## The Threat

The major motivation for Huawei, as a surrogate for the Chinese government, is to support its 100 Year Plan as described by the author, Michael Pillsbury in his book, The Hundred Year Marathon (2016). Huawei is implicitly aligned with this plan that "State-owned enterprises are instructed to acquire assets perceived as valuable by Beijing" (Scissors, 2013 ). It continues a wide-range of acquisitions to include mergers with American and other Western IT companies with the graver concerns by the federal government and the US's IC.

Furthermore, the PLA's Unit 61398 has been extensively analyzed by government and private cybersecurity firms over the past decade. In 2013, **Mandiant** released an exhaustive and authoritative report based upon deep-analysis of code and techniques specific to Unit 61398. The most conclusive statement made was that the "…Communist Party of China is tasking the Chinese People's Liberation Army [Unit 61398 and others] to commit systematic cyber-espionage and data theft…" (Mandiant, 2013, p. 7). It further suggests that some of that training, equipment and expertise is provided by Huawei directly to the PLA.

The **Far Eastern Economic Review** reported "…Huawei received a key contract to supply the PLA's first national telecommunications network" (Ahrens, 2013). These ties point to connections with the Chinese government and the PLA. There is little doubt that China continues aggressive cyber-activities in support of its intentions to increase its economic standing in the world and intrude to the global economic marketplace.

China has demonstrated no desire to quash cyber-espionage activities from within its borders. It is suggested that many Chinese cyber-activities are supported and controlled under the auspices of the Chinese government. The most lucrative target for China, and more specifically Huawei, is the US. Huawei will continue to focus its vast resources against US economic and business entities for the foreseeable future.

Additionally, Huawei has multiple cyber-relevant capabilities to include hardware and software development, IT manufacturing, and in-house technical expertise. However, the major capability afforded Huawei is through its direct backing by the Chinese government. As a mercantile state, the Chinese Communist government has no reason to stop its pursuit of international intellectual property to support its 100 Year Marathon as described in greater detail by Pillsbury (2016). Further, in terms of government contracts and resources, Huawei has powerful direct support from Beijing.

China's intelligence apparatus is vast and vibrant. Access to the Internet as a surreptitious mechanism to hide its activities is also a threat posed by Huawei to subvert the worlds' IT architecture. By leveraging its own infrastructure, in conjunction with the Chinese state, it has near limitless capabilities to disrupt the US and its allies via the Internet; the fears of cyber-espionage are only a small portion of the threat posed by China in the 21st Century.

According to Lachow, Huawei as a complex agent, would require "…a team of individuals (or perhaps multiple teams) with expertise in a number of technical areas…" (Lachow, 2008, p. 444) to exploit the supply chain as well as meet its cyber-espionage collection objectives. Huawei, in coordination with the PLA (or vice versa), has access to formidable resources; "[t]he PLA is reaching out across a wide swath of [the] Chinese civilian sector to meet the intensive requirements necessary to support its burgeoning [Information Warfare] capabilities, incorporating people with specialized skills from commercial industry…" (Krekel, 2009, p. 7).

Huawei should be expected to continue its use the Internet for passive cyber-espionage collection activities; however, it has the potential to engage in more active operations. This could include establishing Command and Control (C2) nodes within its international IT hardware and software sales. Such "infections" pose the greatest risk to the international marketplace. With such access, China continues to represent a formidable offensive threat.


## Vulnerabilities

Huawei has a huge target-set to pursue. With its growth throughout the global IT marketplace, any nation requiring IT products offers a target-rich environment for Huawei to exploit. Targets available to Huawei are wide-ranging and span the entire developed and industrial nations that conduct regular business with China, Huawei, and other Chinese companies.

All countries are potentially exploitable especially in terms of their reliance on the capabilities and vital nature of the Internet. The need for computer hardware and software by developed nations affords a consistent and regular vulnerability. It is also suggested that Huawei personnel have the requisite knowledge and ability to exploit all levels of its manufactured products (and those of its competitors); this capability provides a direct ability to align with Beijing's motivations to become the predominant economic powerhouse of the world.

For example, in terms of cyber-espionage, the **Washington Post** identified in a 2014 article the magnitude of China's intrusions at the time. It was calculated at more than $445 Billion annually "...to the world economy" (Nakashima & Peterson, 2014).  If the allegations against Huawei are true, the potential economic loss to the world could be far greater if Huawei is afforded even greater capacity to process the volumes of exfiltrated data.  The implications would be damage to the global economy more in the trillions of dollars annually in stolen intellectual property and data.

The severest, and more exploitive consequence would be Huawei could have the ability to leverage injected malicious code in its products to eavesdrop on the communications of every device on the Internet.  This could also imply the ability to shutdown portions or the entire Internet because of its control of foundational backbone hardware devices such as routers, switches, and firewalls.  While the ongoing cyber-espionage economic losses to countries are serious, China has the potential to inflict massive offensive harm against countries or groups that in the future it may be in conflict to include the US.

Huawei is a **complex** threat.  Lachow reserves this label to highly coordinated and effective state actors with nearly unlimited resources.  Huawei is such a threat with the obligatory skill-sets to a very diverse and technologically capable adversary. With the presumptive backing of the Chinese government, and its resources, Huawei continues to be a major threat to US and international governments and their respective economies.

While there is no conclusive or even public evidence, that Huawei has injected malicious coding into any of its products, the risk is formidable.  Michael Maloof, a former senior security policy analyst in the Office of the Secretary of Defense, ascribes from sources that "[t]he Chinese government reportedly has "pervasive access" to some 80 percent of the world's communications, thanks to backdoors it has ordered to be installed in devices made by Huawei" (Protalinski, 2012).

Jim Lewis, at  the Center for Strategic and International Studies provided an ominous point of view working with Chinese businesses: "The Chinese will tell you that stealing technology and business secrets [are] a way of building their economy, and that this is important for national security" (Metz, 2013).  The risk to the US's national security, its economic viability, and its critical infrastructure is directly threatened by Huawei. Even at the time of the printing of this book, China, and Huawei, specifically, are identified as key threats. The history of SCRM continues to unfold where there are many legislators and cybersecurity professionals seeking to identify the means to brunt China (as well as other nefarious nation-states from harming or compromising the equipment and data that many of us take for granted. This book provides a 21$^{st}$ Century framework to reasonably and practically implement solutions that mitigate and stop the "bad guys in their tracks.

Ahrens, N. (2013, February). *China's Competitiveness: Myth, Reality and Lessons for the United States and Japan*. Retrieved from Center for Strategic and International Studies: http://csis.org/files/publication/130215_competitiveness_Huawei_casestudy_Web.pdf

Barbozaaug, D. (2010, August 22). *Scrutiny for Chinese Telecom Bid*. Retrieved from New York Times: http://www.nytimes.com/2010/08/23/business/global/23telecom.html?_r=0

DNI. (2015, February 26). *Statement of Record: Worldwide Threat Assessment*. Retrieved from http://www.armed-services.senate.gov/imo/media/doc/Stewart_02-26-15.pdf

Infosec Institute. (2013, October 11). *Hardware attacks, backdoors and electronic component qualification*. Retrieved from Infosec Institute: http://resources.infosecinstitute.com/hardware-attacks-backdoors-and-electronic-component-qualification/

Krekel, B. (2009, October 9). *Capability of the People's Republic of China to Conduct Cyber Warfare and Computer Network Exploitation*. Retrieved from George Washington University: http://nsarchive.gwu.edu/NSAEBB/NSAEBB424/docs/Cyber-030.pdf

Lachow, I. (2008). Cyber Terrorism: Menace or Myth. *Cyber Power*, 19-20.

Mandiant. (2013, February 18). *APT1: Exposing One of China's Cyber Espionage Units*. Retrieved from Mandiant: http://intelreport.mandiant.com/Mandiant_APT1_Report.pdf

Metz, C. (2013, December 31). *U.S. to China: We Hacked Your Internet Gear We Told You Not to Hack*. Retrieved from Wired: http://www.wired.com/2013/12/nsa-cisco-huawei-china/

Nakashima, E., & Peterson, A. (2014, June 9). *Report: Cybercrime and espionage costs $445 billion annually*. Retrieved from Washington Post: http://www.washingtonpost.com/world/national-security/report-cybercrime-and-espionage-costs-445-billion-annually/2014/06/08/8995291c-ecce-11e3-9f5c-9075d5508f0a_story.html

Pillsbury, M. (2015). *The hundred-year marathon: China's secret strategy to replace America as the global superpower*. Henry Holt and Company.

Protalinski, E. (2012, July 14). *Former Pentagon analyst: China has backdoors to 80% of telecoms*. Retrieved from ZDNet: http://www.zdnet.com/article/former-pentagon-analyst-china-has-backdoors-to-80-of-telecoms/

Scissors, D. P. (2013 , May 9). *Chinese Investment in the U.S.: Facts and Motives*. Retrieved from Heritage Society: http://www.heritage.org/research/testimony/2013/05/chinese-investment-in-the-us-facts-and-motives

Simonite, T. (2012, October 9). *Why the United States Is So Afraid of Huawei*. Retrieved from MIT
    Technology Review: http://www.technologyreview.com/news/429542/why-the-united-states-
    is-so-afraid-of-huawei/

US House of Representatives. (2012, October 8). *Investigative Report on the US National Security Issues
    Posed by Chinese Telecommunications Companies Huawei and ZTE*. Retrieved from
    https://intelligence.house.gov/sites/intelligence.house.gov/files/documents/Huawei-
    ZTE%20Investigative%20Report%20(FINAL).pdf

# What is SCRM?

## DEFINITION:

(1). A systematic process for managing supply chain risk by identifying susceptibilities, vulnerabilities, and threats throughout the supply chain and developing mitigation strategies to combat those threats whether presented by the supplier, the supplies product and its subcomponents, or the supply chain (e.g., initial production, packaging, handling, storage, transport, mission operation, and disposal).

(2). The implementation of processes, tools, or techniques to minimize the adverse impact of attacks that allow the adversary to utilize implants or other vulnerabilities inserted prior to installation in order to infiltrate data, or manipulate information technology hardware, software, operating systems, peripherals (information technology products) or services at any point during the life cycle.

(**SOURCE:** https://csrc.nist.gov/glossary/term/supply-chain-risk-management)

Supply chain risks include the insertion of counterfeits, unauthorized production, tampering, theft, insertion of malicious software and hardware (e.g., GPS tracking devices, computer chips, etc.). It also includes poor manufacturing and development practices in the supply chain that introduces or creates risks to the IT system or environment. These risks are realized when threats to the supply chain further create or exploit existing vulnerabilities.

Furthermore, SCRM vulnerabilities if not caught early may take weeks, years, or decades to be launched based upon the objectives and desires of the adversary. It may be difficult to determine whether an event was the direct result of an intentional or unintentional supply chain vulnerability. This may result in an adverse effect on an agencies or businesses operations and missions. This may include degradations to service levels that could lead to customer discontent, theft of intellectual property, or reductions of mission functionality.

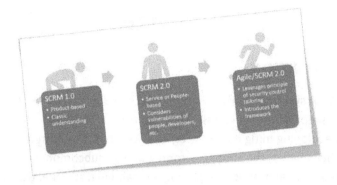

An Evolution to Agile/SCRM

## A Roadmap

The general concept for establishing an effective and repeatable SCRM 1.0 process is outlined in Flowchart 1, *SCRM 1.0 (Product) Process*. The focus is on hardware and software products that constitute most of the current-day SCRM challenge. This will include an initial engineering design that should include requirements documents, technical drawings, and target hardware and software lists that will become a major part of the List of Materials (LOM) [2]. Additionally, these listings become a critical component of any cybersecurity package and are typically part of the System Security Plan (SSP).

The process begins with the classic National Institute of Standards and Technology (NIST) 800-53 approach. The "system owner," working with assigned cybersecurity professionals determine the system categorization [1-maps to Flowchart 1]. The categorization will either be high, moderate, or low. The overall categorization will drive the level of effort and the number of security controls required to protect the system.

*System Categorization* should follow the principles as outlined in NIST Federal Information Processing Standards (FIPS) Publication 199, *Standards for Security Categorization of Federal Information and Information Systems,* February 2004. The following table provides the general descriptions of the "Security Triad" of **Confidentiality**, **Integrity**, and **Availability** (CIA), and the associated definitions based upon their impact levels/dangers to the IT system or environment.

| | POTENTIAL IMPACT | | |
|---|---|---|---|
| Security Objective | LOW | MODERATE | HIGH |
| **Confidentiality** Preserving authorized restrictions on information access and disclosure, including means for protecting personal privacy and proprietary information. [44 U.S.C., SEC. 3542] | The unauthorized disclosure of information could be expected to have a **limited** adverse effect on organizational operations, organizational assets, or individuals. | The unauthorized disclosure of information could be expected to have a **serious** adverse effect on organizational operations, organizational assets, or individuals. | The unauthorized disclosure of information could be expected to have a **severe or catastrophic** adverse effect on organizational operations, organizational assets, or individuals. |
| **Integrity** Guarding against improper information modification or destruction, and includes ensuring information non-repudiation and authenticity. [44 U.S.C., SEC. 3542] | The unauthorized modification or destruction of information could be expected to have a **limited** adverse effect on organizational operations, organizational assets, or individuals. | The unauthorized modification or destruction of information could be expected to have a **serious** adverse effect on organizational operations, organizational assets, or individuals. | The unauthorized modification or destruction of information could be expected to have a **severe or catastrophic** adverse effect on organizational operations, organizational assets, or individuals. |
| **Availability** Ensuring timely and reliable access to and use of information. [44 U.S.C., SEC. 3542] | The disruption of access to or use of information or an information system could be expected to have a **limited** adverse effect on organizational operations, organizational assets, or individuals. | The disruption of access to or use of information or an information system could be expected to have a **serious** adverse effect on organizational operations, organizational assets, or individuals. | The disruption of access to or use of information or an information system could be expected to have a **severe or catastrophic** adverse effect on organizational operations, organizational assets, or individuals. |

(SOURCE: https://nvlpubs.nist.gov/nistpubs/FIPS/NIST.FIPS.199.pdf, p. 6)

The system owner will use the **HIGH WATERMARK** principle in the final selection of the system categorization. The selection will be based upon the highest potential impact from among the three security objectives. The following are simplified examples of how to apply the high watermark principle.

**The system is rated as:**

| Confidentiality | Integrity | Availability | High Watermark Selection |
|:---:|:---:|:---:|:---:|
| H | M | L | H |
| M | L | L | M |
| L | L | L | L |

| H | H | M | H |
|---|---|---|---|
| L | M | H | H |

Typically, a List of Materials (LOM) [2] are generated for the system owner with the assigned project manager and logistics staff supporting the effort. This becomes the basis of the hardware and software list as discussed above and are required for a key artifact of the security accreditation effort, the System Security Plan (SSP).

After the LOM is established and reviewed by the logistics support staff, they will identify key details about the materials [3]. This should include public and known information common to the purchase of the equipment, hardware, software, etc. This will be critical to a Supply Chain Diligence Team (SCDT) review. Logistics will provide details such as:

- Make
- Model
- Manufacturer
- Country of origin
- Memory
- Processing speed
- Chip type
- Third-Party Resellers
- Warranties
- Service Level Agreements (SLA)
- Frequency operation ranges
- Radio Frequency (RF) interference

The SCDT will begin the most vital part of the SCRM 1.0 phase. They will begin by conducting a much deeper analysis of the purchases. This team will conduct a review of by using various public and private databases to determine whether there are any restrictions or concerns about their use based upon the original sensitivity and categorization of the overall system by the system owner and all support staff members. This should include Approved

# SCRM-Product Process

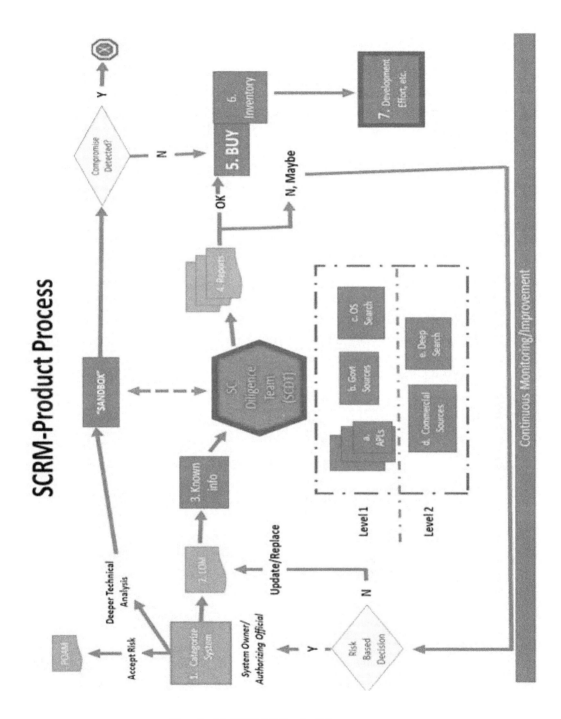

Flowchart 1. SCRM 1.0 (Product) Process

Product Lists (APL), general government sources, and open source searches using basic search engines such as Google®, Bing®, etc.

A Level 2 search is required for a high categorization. This may include access to government restricted classified databases, proprietary commercial sources, or deep/dark web searches requiring greater capabilities and resources by the agency or business. These inputs are used to assess the risk to the overall system. The SCDT will generate reports [4] to other analysts and leaders requiring the information to make future risk-based decisions that may be required later.

Assuming the SCDT do not find any concerns or restrictions about their purchase, the system owner will authorize their buy [5], conduct inventories [6] as they are delivered, and directed to the development effort [7] within a System Development Life Cycle (SDLC) effort typical of current development methodologies and practices.

If the components are found to be either unacceptable or questionable, they will enter the risk-based decision process. If the system owner disapproves of the component, the LOM will be updated, and a suitable replacement identified; it will reenter the process [2] and follow the same workflow.

If the system owner is willing to accept some level of risk, there will be two possible decisions. The system owner will either accept the risk in full, and cybersecurity professionals or other designated IT staff members will create/populate the systems Plan of Action and Milestones (POAM) artifact. The POAM listing will be reviewed *regularly* to determine whether the components risk should continue to be accepted or replaced because of the dangers and risk to the project.

| Category | Suggested POAM Review Cycle |
|---|---|
| | At Least: |
| High | *Every quarter* |
| Moderate | *Every 6 months* |
| Low | *Annually* |

If desired, a deeper technical analysis may occur by certified/qualified individuals usually from the SCDT. Third-party assessors with the requisite skills and tools may also be used to determine the risk posed by the product purchased. This deeper analysis should occur in a designated "sandbox" environment not connected to any active or operational networks. Assessment may use software and hardware designed to identify any malicious code, improper transmissions to outside Internet Protocol (IP) addresses or ports, etc. The designated experts from the SCDT should play an integral part of any reports to determine risk posed.

If a compromise is detected, it is highly recommended that the product be removed and designated as a threat. The business or agency should notify the appropriate agency in accordance with its Incident Response Plan (IRP); it is vital that the results of the technical analysis is shared as widely as possible to notify and update databases supporting the SCRM process. If no compromise is detected, and the system owner approves, the component may be bought [5] to meet the system needs of the organization.

## Continuous Monitoring v. Continual Improvement

The final and long-term effort should include continuous monitoring. Continuous Monitoring (ConMon) should be an active part of the overall cybersecurity protection effort. ConMon should reassess over time the state of IT purchases to identify and determine any changes during the life of the system. It is especially critical for those products that have received a POAM, and their threat to the system needs be minimized based upon its sensitivity to the organization. There are several sub-components that also comprise the ConMon effort to include, but not limited to:

- Vendor changes
- Software Patching
- Anti-virus/Anti-malware updates
- Operating System changes
- Changes in multi-factor access (e.g., biometric upgrades, etc.)

Continuous improvement should also be the goal of leadership to improve the SCRM process. This may include adding additional logistics reviews, enhanced skills training for SCDT personnel, or updated tools to better protect the system. Continuous improvement should include recurring lessons learned meetings and repositories to enhance the organizations knowledge management efforts. Reports, spreadsheets, databases, and repositories should be integral tools to ensure improvement of the supply chain protection efforts.

# NIST 800-171 Applicability to Future Contract Awards

## Expectations

In 2019, the expectation is that the United States (US) federal government will formally expand the National Institute of Standards and Technology (NIST) Special Publication (SP) 800-171, revision 1, *Protecting Unclassified Information in Nonfederal Information Systems and Organizations* cybersecurity technical publication will apply to the entirety of the federal government. It will **mandate** and **enforce** that any college or university accepting taxpayer dollars will be required to be fully compliant with NIST 800-171. The Federal Acquisition Regulation (FAR) Committee's Case # 2017-016 had an original suspense date of March 2018; that date has come and gone. The latest and expected timeframe for any final decision is unknown as of the date of the print of this book; however, colleges and universities are already mandated by the Department of Education (ED) to adopt and use NIST 800-171 as part of already promulgated rules to institutions of higher education.

*While NIST 800-series Cybersecurity publications tell a College or University (C/U) "what" is required, they do not necessarily help in telling "how" to meet the 110 security control requirements of NIST 800-171. The number of security controls may further increase based upon the actual or perceived threats to a federal agency, but at this time, the understanding and execution of the 110 controls is vital to protecting privacy information to include Controlled Unclassified Information (CUI).*

---

## *Colleges and Universities (C/U) should always confirm control requirements with their respective Contract Offices or Department of Education*

---

This book is created to help C/Us in meeting this universal cybersecurity and contracting requirement. It is intended to assist C/Us and their Information Technology (IT) staffs' on how to best address the challenges of meeting the 2016 National Institute of Standards and Technology (NIST) 800-171, revision 1. This further includes compliance with the Federal Acquisition Regulation (FAR) clause 52.204-21 and its companion DOD supplement, the Defense Federal Acquisition Regulation Supplement (DFARS), and its specific clause, 252.204-7012.

Additionally, this book is dedicated and created to give C/Us and their IT staffs a substantive start-point. It is designed to walk through the security controls in enough detail to ensure authorization to operate and conduct regular business, goods, and services, (to include federally funded research and activities) with the US federal government. This approach is offered in anticipation of a federal-wide requirement for C/Us attempting to show a "good-faith" representation of meeting the new NIST 800-171 requirements.

NIST 800-171 applies to **prime and subcontractors**. There are three core contractual obligations:

1. "Adequately safeguard" Controlled Unclassified Information (CUI), and if working with the Department of Defense (DOD), Covered/Critical Defense Information (CDI).

2. Provide timely cyber-incident reporting to the government when a IT network breach is identified; typically, within 72 hours or sooner.

3. If operating with a Cloud Service Provider (CSP), "adequate" security needs to be demonstrated; usually through a contract with the CSP that shows that they are providing adequate security to provide data protection as a third-party service provider. A contract or Service Level Agreement (SLA) should show the C/U is executing sound cybersecurity diligence to government Contract Officers (CO).

What is "adequate security?" **Adequate security** is defined by "compliance" with the 110 NIST 800-171 security controls, and when the C/U is issued an award. It will also be considered adequate upon an authorization issued to the C/U by the designated CO. This does not mean all security controls are in effect, *but where a deviation is needed, a Plan of Action and Milestones (POAM) is provided.*

A POAM is required as part of the official submission package to the government. It should identify why the C/U cannot currently address the control, and when it expects to resolve the control. (See the supplementary guide: *Writing an Effective Plan of Action & Milestones (POAM) available on Amazon® for further details.*)

The C/U is also required to provide timely cyber-incident reporting to the government when a breach into its network has occurred. The DOD requirement, for example, is that the notification to the government is done within 72 hours upon *recognition* of a security incident. (See the chapter on the Incident Response (IR) control family).

Additionally, the US Government may require the C/U to notify cybersecurity support and response elements within the federal government. This may include the Department of Homeland Security's (DHS) US Computer Emergency Response Team (US-CERT) (https://www.us-cert.gov/ ), the Department of Education (ED), or other like agency within the government.

Changing federal cybersecurity contract requirements are also taking into consideration the vast moves within the public and private sectors into cloud services. Typically, the security protections would be found in any contracts or SLA between the C/U and the CSP. These are normally sufficient evidence for the government.

The good news regarding CSPs are there are many current CSPs that are already in compliance with the government's Federal Risk and Authorization Management Program (FedRAMP). Being FEDRAMP-compliant prior to final submission of the NIST 800-171 Body of Evidence (BOE) will reduce the challenges of using an uncertified CSP; plan accordingly if considering moving part or all the C/U 's operations into the "cloud."

## Consequences of Non-compliance

There are several major consequences contractors and their subcontractors need to consider if either unable to meet or maintain their compliance. This can include several serious consequences and it is vital the C/U stays current regarding any changes in their cybersecurity posture. Stay constantly current regarding any new NIST 800-171 direction in general, or specific to the agency being supported. Failing to stay current with the Contract office may jeopardize C/U relationships with the government. These consequences may include:

- Impact to Future Contract Selection. This may be as basic as a temporary disbarment from federal contract work. It could also include permanent measures by government to suspend a C/U for a much longer period. Furthermore, the government could pursue the C/U for fraud or clear misrepresentation of their security posture to the US Government. This most likely would occur when a cybersecurity **incident** occurs within the C/U's network. This most likely would result in government appointed third-party assessor that would determine whether there was a willful disregard for NIST 800-171 and any associated FAR/DFARS clauses. *Remember*, the C/U will always be assessed against the following criteria:
  - o Was there **adequate security** in place prior and during the incident?

- Were the protections adequately established based upon a **good-faith** effort by the C/U to protect CUI/CDI?

- <u>Assessments Initiated by the Government.</u>  At this phase, the Government will have unfettered access to determine culpability of the incident and whether it further brought harm against the government and its agencies.  Cooperation is a key obligation and hiding the incident may have worse impacts than not reporting the intrusion.

- <u>A POAM will be required.</u>  The government will mandate a POAM be developed to address the finding.  This should be a good effort to identify interim milestones with final and planned completion dates to ensure a situation will not reoccur.  (See the supplement: *Writing an Effective Plan of Action & Milestones:* https://www.amazon.com/Writing-Effective-Plan-Action-Milestones-ebook/dp/B07H2M3F2M/ref=sr_1_2?ie=UTF8&qid=1536967628&sr=8-2&keywords=POAM )

- <u>Loss of Contract.</u>  Worse case, the Contract Officer may determine that the C/U failed to meet the cybersecurity requirements.  The results of that determination most likely will result in cancelation of the contract for *cause*.

## The Likely Course: FAR Clause 52.204-21

For <u>very basic</u> safeguarding of contractor information systems that process, store, or transmit federal "contract information," expect this clause will be modified to reduce several of the specific NIST 800-171 security controls.  A pared down selection of controls would be used in the early stages of NIST 800-171 implementation and transition for a federal agency. FAR 52.204-21 may be modified to about fifteen (15) "basic" cybersecurity controls for the contractor's information system. This will apply most typically to "federal contract information" where a C/U clearly stores, processes, or transmits federal data. The specific language is:

> *"Information, not intended for public release, that is provided by or generated for the Government under a contract to develop or deliver a product or service to the Government, but not including information provided to the public (such as on public Web sites) or simple transactional information, such as necessary to process payments."*

This clause will <u>not</u> require all 110 security controls and is expected to reduce or minimize the following types of associated controls:

1) Cybersecurity training requirements

2) Two-factor authentication (2FA)
3) Detailed system control descriptions
4) Cybersecurity incidents or breach notifications

Expect few federal agencies to apply this clause long-term since it opens the federal agency to both public and congressional scrutiny. Expect this to be applied as a short-term solution until such time a future contract modification occurs, and the agency is more confident in its understanding and application of NIST 800-171.

This book is applicable for FAR 52.204-21 implementation scenario. It can be used to answer the expected 15 security controls as identified in subsequent chapters of this book. Verify the actual required security controls with the Contract Office. It is important to confirm the needed control explanations as described later in the specified in later chapters and their respective control family.

## What's the minimum proof of a C/U 's cybersecurity posture?

The basis of NIST 800-171 is that C/U provide adequate security on all covered contractor Information Systems (IS). Typically, the minimum requirement to demonstrate control implementation is through **documentation**. Another term that is used throughout this book is an **artifact**. An artifact is any representation to a Contract Office or independent third-party assessor that shows compliance with specific security controls. It is a major part of the proof that a C/U owner would provide to the federal government.

The common term for the collection of all applications and supporting artifacts is the Body of Evidence (BOE). The major items required for the BOE includes three major items:

1. **C/U Policy or Procedure.** For this book, these terms are used interchangeably. Essentially any direction provided to internal employees and subcontractors that are enforceable under US labor laws and Human Resource (HR) direction. It is recommended that such a policy or procedure artifact be a singular collection of how the C/U addresses each of the 110 security controls.

---

*All cybersecurity-related policy or procedure requirements are best captured in single policy or procedure guide. This should address the controls aligned with the security control families*

---

2. **System Security Plan (SSP).** This is a standard cybersecurity document. It describes the C/U's overall IT infrastructure to include hardware and software lists. Where

appropriate, suggestions of additional artifacts that should be included in this document and duplicated into a standard SSP format will be recommended. (See *https://cybersentinel.tech for the latest template).*

A *free* 36-minute introduction to the SSP is currently available on Udemy.com at https://www.udemy.com/system-security-plan-ssp-for-nist-800-171-compliance/.

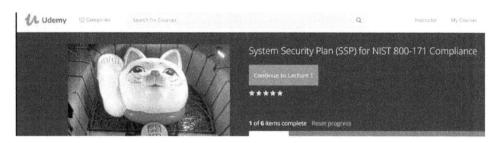

3.  **Plans of Action and Milestones (POAM).** This describes any control that the C/U cannot fix or fully demonstrate its full compliance. It provides an opportunity for a C/U to delay addressing a difficult to implement technical solution or because cost may be prohibitive.

    POAMs should always have an expected completion date and defined interim milestones that describes the actions leading to a full resolution or implementation of the control. *POAMs typically should not be for more than a year, however, a critical hint, a C/U can request an extension multiple times if unable to fully meet the control.*

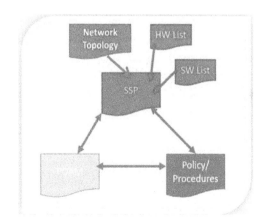

**The Major Artifacts Required by the Federal Government under NIST 800-171**

*When working with the government, being simple and consistent always helps through a very young and less-than-defined process*

Other artifacts that will occasionally be discussed, but no less important, are the SSP and POAM. These will be major portions of the submitted BOE to the government. Artifacts are designed to support assertions of completeness and this book, for example, may include "screen captures" as one of many proofs that a control is met; all modern Operating Systems (OS) include a "print screen" function where the text or image is captured, placed in temporary computer memory and can be inserted into a document application. This can then easily be provided to a CO or a security control assessor in the form of either a soft or hard copy artifact. IT personnel should use this function to show, for example, policy settings or system logging (audit) data. When in doubt, always have some form of graphical representation to show the government.

The POAM will be used where the C/U cannot meet or address the control either for technical reasons, "we don't have a Data at Rest (DAR) encryption application," or cost, "we plan to purchase the DAR solution No Later Than April 1, 2019." POAMs should include milestones; milestones should describe what will be accomplished overtime to prepare for the full implementation of the control in the future. What will the C/U do in the interim to address the control? This could include, for example, other mitigation responses of using improved physical security controls, such as a 24-7 guard force, the addition of a steel-door to prevent entry to the main computer servers or improved and enforceable policies that have explicit repercussions upon personnel.

POAMs will always have a defined end date. Typically, it is either within 90 days, six months, or a year in length. One year should be the maximum date; however, the C/U, as part of this fledgling process, can request an extension to the POAM based on the "planned" end date; RMF affords flexibilities. Don't be afraid to exercise and use POAMs as appropriate. (See Access Control (AC) for a sample template).

# DOD Cybersecurity gets (even more) Serious

In 2014, DOD adopted the overall NIST RMF 800-series as its cybersecurity standard. In 2017, it officially required its contract workforce to specifically meet the NIST 800-171 requirement. The overall direction has become the current DOD guidance to more effectively protect its own critical IT data and infrastructures, and to expand beyond its DOD boundaries to protect *its* data transmitted into the private contractor sector.

NIST 800-171 will be a challenge for companies, college, and universities wanting to continue or begin commercial ventures with the government. This book is committed to providing a rational approach that novice through expert IT personnel can effectively employ to answer the 110 security controls. It is through a "good-faith" effort on the part of the C/U that is expected to protect sensitive data types such as CUI and CDI.

This is a how-to book. It was originally based upon the DOD's current execution of NIST 800-171, but also the federal-wide government enactment of NIST 800-171. NIST 800-171 revision 1 was the first attempt for DOD that applies to vendors and contractors to ensure CUI/CDI is properly protected from threats. DOD is attempting to ensure a basic effort is executed to protect a company's own internal CUI as well as co-mingled DOD information that is created as part of the business 's normal operations.

As of December 31, 2017, any company wishing to do business with DOD is required to meet the **110** NIST-based security controls. Companies can implement these security solutions either directly or by using outside, third-party, "managed services" to satisfy the protection requirements of Controlled Unclassified Information (CUI)/Covered Defense Information (CDI). NIST publications while not previously mandatory for "nonfederal entities," NIST 800-171 rev. 1, is the first time that a federal agency has mandated nonfederal agencies, vis a vis, private companies, comply with this federal-specific publication.

"Nonfederal" organizations, such as company or C/U, and their internal IT systems processing, storing, or transmitting CUI/CDI will be required to comply with NIST 800-171. In the case of DOD, that suggestion is *now* mandatory.

*CUI and CDI are not considered national security level information as most typical within the DOD such as **Confidential**, **Secret**, or **Top Secret**. The former DOD terminology for CUI or CDI was predominantly categorized as **For Official Use Only** (FOUO). This data is considered sensitive, but not requiring more stringent security or control mechanisms as with national security information. Basic CUI/CDI may include employee records, Personal Health Information (PHI), or Personally Identifiable Information (PII) protected by federal and state laws. CDI is more specific to the operational and support functions required by DOD to perform its national mission.*

The **110** explicit security controls from NIST 800-171 are extracted from NIST's core cyber security document, NIST 800-53, *Security and Privacy Controls for Federal Information Systems and Organizations*, which are considered vital for DOD.

This is a highly pared down set of controls to meet the security requirement based on approximately 800 potential controls offered from NIST 800-53; this is a more expansive set of controls used by DOD to protect all its combat and general IT support systems. This includes everything from its jet fighters to its vast personnel databases.

---

# People-Process-Technology (PPT) Model

This book focuses C/U, and their IT support staff, to meet both the minimum and more complete suggested answers for each of the specified controls. C/U fortunately only need to focus on how to best address these controls in a "minimal" nature and ensure concurrence from the federal government that the C/U has positive control of its security boundaries where its mission systems and data reside. Furthermore, it is more thoughtfully intended to help the C/U protect its private and sensitive data.

The **People, Process, and Technology (PPT) Model** is the recommended guidance for answering many of the controls within NIST 800-171. While all solutions will not necessarily require a **technological** answer, consideration of the **people** (e.g., who? what skill sets? etc.) and **process** (e.g., notifications to senior management, action workflows, etc.) will meet many of the response requirements. Refer to Control 3.6.1 that provides example responses that could be offered when applying the People-Process-Technology (PPT) model. The best responses will typically include the types and kinds of people assigned to oversee the control, the process or procedures that identify the workflow that will ensure that the control is met, and in some cases, the technology that will answer the control in part or in full.

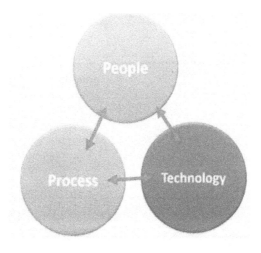

**PPT Model**

# All Things Considered

## Getting into a cybersecurity mind-set

The focus is to provide the mental approach and technical understanding of what the control is (and what it is not). The first paragraph describes a MINIMUM ANSWER. This is what is needed to prepare a basic answer for a minimal and acceptable level of response. Mainly, these solutions require policy or procedural documents that describe to the government how the C/U will ensure this control will be met; if just trying to get through the process expeditiously, this paragraph will be enough to secure an approval.

If there is a greater desire to understand the process further and demonstrate a more substantial solution, the paragraph, MORE COMPLETE ANSWER is designed to provide more depth. It is intended to more completely describe to the C/U how to better show an understanding to the federal government its implementation of NIST 800-171.

Also, for clarification, the *Basic Security Requirement* **heading** is what is typically described as the **Common Control** for the control family. It is best just to understand it is the major control for the respective control family. The *Derived Security Requirements* can be considered more as supplemental and "more granular" requirements for the "parent" control. Depending on the types and kinds of data stored, these controls in the more *classic* NIST 800-53 publication can include hundreds of other controls; the US Government has fortunately deemed only 110 controls as necessary.

| FAMILY | FAMILY |
|---|---|
| (AC) Access Control | (MP) Media Protection |
| (AT) Awareness and Training | (PS) Personnel Security |
| (AU) Audit and Accountability | (PP) Physical Protection |
| (CM) Configuration Management | (RA) Risk Assessment |
| (IA) Identification and Authentication | (SA) Security Assessment |
| (IR) Incident Response | (SC) System and Communications Protection |
| (MA) Maintenance | (SI) System and Information Integrity |

NIST 800-171 SECURITY REQUIREMENT FAMILIES

## Tailoring-out Controls Possibilities

The 2016 version update to NIST 800-171, revision 1, provides a less-than adequate direction on the matter of **control tailoring**. It states in its Appendix E that there are three primary criteria for the removal of a security control (or control enhancement) from consideration and inclusion within the NIST 800-171 BOE:

• **The control is uniquely federal (i.e., primarily the responsibility of the federal government):** The government directly provides the control to the C/U. While possible, expect this not typically to occur.

• **The control is not directly related to protecting the confidentiality of CUI/CDI:** This will also not apply since all these controls were originally chosen to protect the confidentiality of all CUI/CDI. That's why this book exists to explain better how to address these controls which are for the most part all required.

• **The control is expected to be routinely satisfied by Nonfederal Organizations (NFO) without specification:** In other words, the control is expected to be met by the NFO, i.e., the C/U (you and your IT team.)

Tailoring is allowed and recommended where appropriate. Within the NIST cybersecurity framework, the concept of **tailoring-out** of a control is desirable where technically or operationally it cannot be reasonably applied. This will require technical certainty that the control is Non-Applicable (N/A). Under this opportunity, if the C/U 's IT architecture does not contain within its **security boundary** the technology where such a control would be required to be applied then the control is identified as N/A.

For example, where the C/U has no Wi-Fi network in its security boundary, it can advise the government that any controls addressing the security of Wi-Fi networks would be an N/A control. The C/U cannot nor have reason to implement these security controls because it currently doesn't allow Wi-Fi networks or any presence of such equipment such as Wi-Fi routers, antennas, etc. The control would be marked as **compliant** and annotated as N/A at the time of the self-assessment. It would still be required to identify that Wi-fi is not currently authorized in the C/U's cybersecurity procedure guide or policy to properly document its absence as a suggested best-practice approach for the submitted BOE.

The following Wi-fi security controls most likely can be tailored-out specific to the C/U 's existing IT infrastructure if there are no Wi-fi networks or devices.

---

*3.1.16 Authorize wireless access prior to allowing such connections.*
*3.1.17 Protect wireless access using authentication and encryption.*

---

## *Tailoring-out can be your friend*

---

# How to use this book

In June 2018, the NIST issued NIST 800-171A, **"A**ssessing Security Requirements for Controlled Unclassified Information."** It increased the challenges and complexity of the current federal, *and especially* DOD efforts, to better secure the cybersecurity environment. It added another 298 sub-controls (SUB CTRL), also described within the cybersecurity community as a Control Correlation Identifier (CCI). The *CCI* provides a standard identifier and description for each of the singular, actionable statements that comprise a cybersecurity control or cybersecurity best practice. CCI bridges the gap between high-level policy expressions and low-level technical implementations. CCI allows a security requirement that is expressed in a high-level policy framework to be decomposed and explicitly associated with the low-level security setting(s) that must be assessed to determine compliance with the objectives of that specific security control.

The ability to trace security requirements from their origin (e.g., regulations, cybersecurity frameworks, etc.) to their low-level implementation allows organizations to readily demonstrate to multiple cybersecurity compliance frameworks. CCI also provides a means to objectively rollup and compare related compliance assessment results across disparate technologies.

We are issuing this edition to better address our work and hope to better assist in this change that will have limited impacts to you and your C/U or agency. This version will leverage the original version of "NIST 800-171: Beyond DOD," available on Amazon, and provides more details of "how" to answer these additional sub-controls.

The effort here will primarily focus on using "examination" primarily to meet the control while suggesting, where appropriate, the use of "testing" and "interviews" are a better approach to answering the sub-controls; most of recommended approaches will be based upon updates to the C/U's policy or procedure documents specific to computer security within their respective security boundary.

We have modified the original NIST 800-171A sub-control charts and have added an additional column to explain suggested approaches to answer the sub-control for a minimal 'compliant' status. We will not attempt to do more than that for the purposes of this edition.

The generalized assessment from NIST 800-171A only describes an expanded framework and a starting point for developing more specific procedures to assess the CUI security requirements in NIST 800-171 revision 1. *It does not add new controls, it only provides more detailed enhancements to the base control. There are still 110 controls.*

Organizations have the flexibility to specialize their assessment procedures by selecting the specific assessment methods and the set of assessment artifacts to achieve the assessment objectives. There is no expectation that all assessment methods and all artifacts will be used for every assessment. The assessment procedures and methods can be applied using multiple approaches to include self-assessment or independent, third-party assessments. Assessments may also be performed by sponsoring organizations (e.g., government agencies); such approaches may be specified in contracts or in agreements by participating parties. Every effort has been attempted in this edition to provide additional information for the sub-control as needed.

Furthermore, assessments can be conducted by systems' developers, integrators, assessors, system owners, or their respective security staffs. Assessment teams combine available system information. System assessments can be used to compile and evaluate the evidence needed by organizations and to help determine the effectiveness of the safeguards implemented to protect CUI.

The following key is provided to add brevity.

| ACRONYM | MEANING | DESCRIPTION |
|---------|---------|-------------|
| NCR | No Change Required | The description and information in the base control is still correct and there is no further need to modify the original administrative (policy) or technical recommendations. |
| P | Policy or Procedure | Requires an addition to the C/U 's policy document to answer the sub-control; descriptions or examples are suggested as the "recommended approach" column. |

| | | |
|---|---|---|
| T | Technical solution is needed | Identifies a technical solution is further needed to answer the control AND/OR mitigate (reduces) the vulnerability, but not necessarily completely. |
| PO | Plan of Action & Milestones | The suggestion here is for C/U, where the control appears to be technically difficult to implement, a POAM should be formulated; if able to address, it is always the *preferred* approach to answering any security control. |
| W | Waiver or Risk Acceptance | There are some situations—very long-term—where a waiver or risk acceptance, by the C/U, is a mechanism to accept risk for a control difficult to implement for several years due to lack of expertise, technologically or budget to fulfill the requirement |

For the purposes of this book, the interview method is NOT recommended. While it can be used to verify the quality and completeness of documentation to include, for example, user and administrator manuals it should not be used on its own. We primarily recommend that document reviews with subsequent technical testing should be the two primary assessment methods. Technical testing of documented processes with associated artifacts are the best approach for a large majority of the controls cited with NIST 800-171.

---

## Good Processes Provide Good Test Artifact Outputs— If there are none, then the process has NO value

---

# ACCESS CONTROL (AC)
## *The most technical, complex, and vital*

Access Control (AC) is probably the most technical and most vital security control family within the cybersecurity process. It is designed to focus computer support personnel, System Administrators (SA), or similar IT staff, on the technical security protections of critical data. This will include any CUI/CDI and internal sensitive data maintained by the C/U 's IT infrastructure and maintained by the C/U as part of doing C/U with the government. If making investments in cybersecurity infrastructure upgrades, the *AC control will provide the greatest Return on Investment*.

Also, it is important to confirm whether either a technical solution is not already embedded in the current IT system. Many times, controls are ignored, captured by policy, or a POAM is developed, even though some base capabilities to address the control are already resident in the base system or more particularly within the network Operating System (OS). Also, check for accessory applications provided by the OS manufacturer to determine whether a no-cost solution is already resident. Ask the IT staff to confirm whether there is an existing technical solution as part of the system to avoid spending additional dollars for capabilities already in place.

Where cost is currently prohibitive to implement, a POAM is an acceptable but temporary solution. If unable to address the control during the C/U 's "self-assessment" effort, then be prepared to formulate a Plans of Action and Milestone (POAM). (***Writing an Effective POAM*** is a current supplement to this book and may be found on Amazon®).

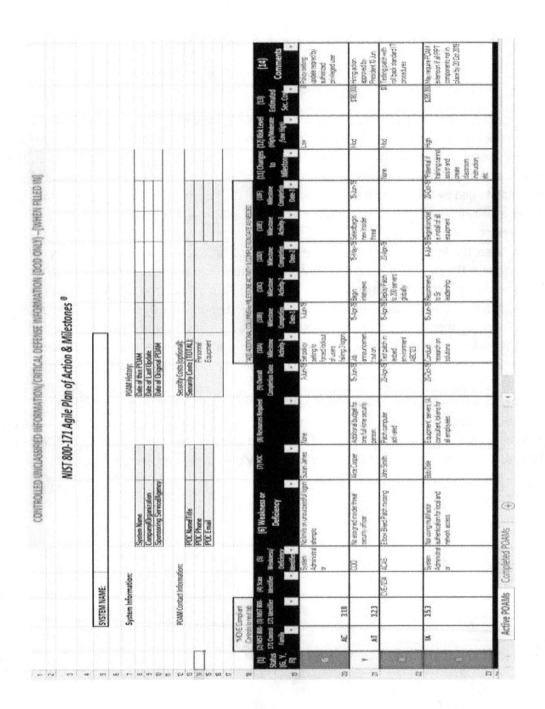

**Sample POAM Template**

(This template can be found at https://cybersentinel.tech in the Cyber-Shop)

**Basic Security Requirements:**

## 3.1.1 Limit information system access to authorized users, processes acting on behalf of authorized users, or devices (including other information systems).

MINIMUM ANSWER: Address this control in the C/U policy/procedural document. (See example procedure below).

It should identify the types of users and what level of access they are authorized. Typically, there are **general users** who have regular daily access to the C/U system data, and **elevated/privileged users**.

Elevated/privileged users are usually limited to, for example, System Administrators (SA), Database Administrators (DBA), and other designated Help Desk IT support staff personnel who manage the back-office care of the system; these users usually have **root access**. Root access provides what is more typically described as **super-user** access. These individuals should be highly and regularly screened. These individuals need to be regularly assessed or audited by senior C/U designated personnel.

MORE COMPLETE ANSWER: This should include screen captures that show a sample of employees and their types and kinds of access rights. This could include their read, write, edit, delete, etc., **rights** typically controlled by an assigned SA.

We have provided an example of a suggested procedure for this control:

> EXAMPLE PROCEDURE: *The C/U has defined two types of authorized users. There are **general users**, those that require normal daily access to C/U automated resources, and **privileged users**, employees with elevated privileges required to conduct regular back-office care and maintenance of C/U assets and Information Technology (IT) systems. Access to the C/U 's [example] financial, ordering and human resource systems will be restricted to those general users with a need, based upon their duties, to access these systems. Immediate supervisors will validate their need and advise the IT Help Desk to issue appropriate access credentials [login identification and password] after completing "Cybersecurity Awareness Training." User credentials will not be shared and...."*

| ASSESSMENT OBJECTIVE *Determine if:* | | |
|---|---|---|
| **SUB-CTRL** | *DESCRIPTION* | RECOMMENDED APPROACH |
| **3.1.1[a]** | *Authorized users are identified.* | NCR |
| **3.1.1[b]** | *Processes acting on behalf of authorized users are identified.* | *P-Processes need to by further defined. This should include access to major applications and their functionality, e.g., finance for finance personnel only, contracting for contract personnel only; also,* |

| | | some supervisors will require access to these functional "processes" for oversight purposes. |
|---|---|---|
| 3.1.1[c] | Devices (and other systems) authorized to connect to the system are identified. | SSP-Should identify all devices internal to the security boundary as main source document. |
| 3.1.1[d] | System access is limited to authorized users. | NCR |
| 3.1.1[e] | System access is limited to processes acting on behalf of authorized users. | P-Update policy document that states "system access is limited to processes acting on behalf of authorized users." |
| 3.1.1[f] | System access is limited to authorized devices (including other systems). | P/SSP-State in policy document; should align with SSP. |

**ASSESSMENT METHOD AND OBJECTS**

Examine: [SELECT FROM: Access control policy; procedures addressing account management; system security plan; system design documentation; system configuration settings and associated documentation; list of active system accounts and the name of the individual associated with each account; notifications or records of recently transferred, separated, or terminated employees; list of conditions for group and role membership; list of recently disabled system accounts along with the name of the individual associated with each account; access authorization records; account management compliance reviews; system monitoring records; system audit logs and records; list of devices and systems authorized to connect to organizational systems; other relevant documents or records].

## 3.1.2 Limit information system access to the types of transactions and functions that authorized users are permitted to execute.

MINIMUM ANSWER: Address this control in the C/U policy/procedural document. It should identify the types of transactions and what level is allowed for authorized users. Elevated or privileged users have access to back-office maintenance and care of the network such as account creation, database maintenance, etc.; privileged users can also have general access, but different logins and passwords should segregate their privileges for audit purposes.

MORE COMPLETE ANSWER: This could include a screen capture that shows a sample of employees and their types and kinds of rights. This would include their read, write, edit, delete, etc., rights typically controlled by assigned SA. The SA should be able to provide the hardcopy printouts for inclusion into the final submission packet to the contract office or their designated recipient.

| ASSESSMENT OBJECTIVE Determine if: | | |
|---|---|---|
| **SUB-CTRL** | **DESCRIPTION** | **RECOMMENDED APPROACH** |
| 3.1.2[a] | The types of transactions and functions that authorized users are permitted to execute are defined. | NCR |
| 3.1.2[b] | System access is limited to the defined types of transactions and functions for authorized users. | NCR |

## Derived (Supplemental) Security Requirements:

## 3.1.3 Control the flow of CUI flowing the approved authorizations.

MINIMUM ANSWER:  Companies typically use **flow control** policies and technologies to manage the movement of CUI/CDI throughout the IT architecture; flow control is based on the types of information.

In terms of procedural updates, discussion of the C/U  documents should address several areas of concern: 1) That only authorized personnel within the C/U  with the requisite need-to-know are provided access; 2) appropriate security measures are in place to include encryption while Data is in Transit (DIT); 3) what are the procedures for handling internal employees who violate these C/U rules?; and, 4) how does the C/U  alert the federal government if there is external access (hackers) to its IT infrastructure and its CUI/CDI?

MORE COMPLETE ANSWER: Addressing this control can further be demonstrated by implementing training (See Awareness and Training (AT) control) as a form of **mitigation**; mitigation are other supporting efforts, not just technical, that can reduce the effects if a threat exploits this control.  The C/U could also include risk from insider threats (See Control 3.2.3 for discussion of "insider threat.") by requiring employees to complete Non-disclosure (NDA) and non-compete agreements (NCA). These added measures *reduce or mitigate the risk to the IT infrastructure*. They should also address employees that depart, resign, or are terminated by the C/U; the consideration is for disgruntled employees that may depart the C/U with potentially sensitive CUI/CDI.

Flow control could also be better shown to a federal government assessor in terms of a technical solution.  This could be further demonstrated by using encryption for DIT and Data at Rest (DAR).  These encryption requirements within NIST 800-171 necessitate differing technical solutions, and Federal Information Processing Standards (FIPS) 140-2 compliance; see Control 3.13.11 for more detail.

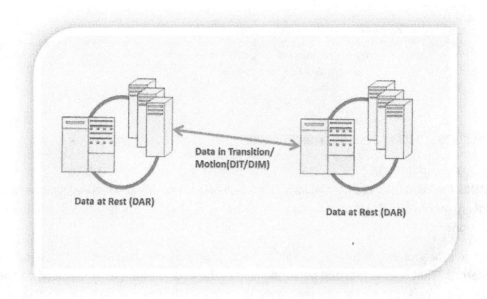

**Data at Rest (DAR) versus Data in Transit/Motion (DIT/DIM) Conceptual Diagram**

The answer could also include weekly reviews of access logs. Typically, IT support personnel or the SA would conduct recurring audits. If anomalies are detected, what is the procedure to alert senior management to personnel attempting access to CUI/CDI and other sensitive data? This offers a greater demonstration of C/U security measures to government representatives.

| ASSESSMENT OBJECTIVE: *Determine if:* | | |
|---|---|---|
| **SUB-CTRL** | *DESCRIPTION* | **RECOMMENDED APPROACH** |
| **3.1.3[a]** | *Information flow control policies are defined.* | NCR |
| **3.1.3[b]** | *Methods and enforcement mechanisms for controlling the flow of CUI are defined.* | NCR (P-especially FIPS 140-2 encryption standards). |
| **3.1.3[c]** | *Designated sources and destinations (e.g., networks, individuals, and devices) for CUI within the system and between interconnected systems are identified.* | P/SSP-Add an update to policy/procedure document and a "data flow" diagram to SSP that describes what the flow from the originator to destination involves. At each source or destination identify whether the data is encrypted or not. |
| **3.1.3[d]** | *Authorizations for controlling the flow of CUI are defined.* | NCR |
| **3.1.3[e]** | *Approved authorizations for controlling the flow of CUI are enforced.* | P-Updates to the policy should identify the individual or body that can make approved changes to "data flow." |

## 3.1.4 Separate the duties of individuals to reduce the risk of malevolent activity without collusion.

MINIMUM ANSWER: This should be described in the C/U cybersecurity procedural document and should identify roles and responsibilities of how oversight will be executed. When this is difficult, based on the size and limited IT personnel, a POAM is highly recommended.

The POAM should suggest other ways used to mitigate such a **risk**, and potentially look at both human and automated means to better address in the future.

MORE COMPLETE ANSWER: Individuals should be assigned *in-writing* and their roles and responsibilities. This could also include the reporting thresholds of unauthorized activities and who is alerted internal threats; this would better provide a more defined solution. It also could address Human Resource (HR) challenges when such incidents occur and provide a means of action against violators of C/U policy.

**ASSESSMENT OBJECTIVE** *Determine if:*

| SUB-CTRL | DESCRIPTION | RECOMMENDED APPROACH |
|---|---|---|
| 3.1.4[a] | *The duties of individuals requiring separation are defined.* | NCR |
| 3.1.4[b] | *Responsibilities for duties that require separation are assigned to separate individuals.* | NCR |
| 3.1.4[c] | *Access privileges that enable individuals to exercise the duties that require separation are granted to separate individuals.* | NCR |

## 3.1.5 Employ the principle of least privilege, including for specific security functions and privileged accounts.

MINIMUM ANSWER: The principle of least privilege is an important cybersecurity tenet. The concept of least privilege is about allowing only authorized access for users and processes that they have direct responsibility.  It is limited to only a necessary level of access to accomplish tasks for specific C/U functions. This should be described in the C/U cybersecurity policy document.  This should also be part of basic user agreements to include what is described in government terminology an **Acceptable Use Policy** (AUP).

MORE COMPLETE ANSWER: Much like the controls described above, a sampling of employees' print-outs or screen captures could show selected and authorized individual rights.  A sampling, especially of privileged users, and their assigned roles within the C/U 's IT infrastructure would be a target of potential third-party government assessors.  This would be used by assessors to support the developing NIST 800-171 certification process.

| ASSESSMENT OBJECTIVE *Determine if:* | | |
|---|---|---|
| **SUB-CTRL** | *DESCRIPTION* | **RECOMMENDED APPROACH** |
| **3.1.5[a]** | *Privileged accounts are identified.* | P-Should have a list of privileged users as an ongoing artifact. |
| **3.1.5[b]** | *Access to privileged accounts is authorized in accordance with the principle of least privilege.* | NCR |
| **3.1.5[c]** | *Security functions are identified.* | NCR |
| **3.1.5[d]** | *Access to security functions is authorized in accordance with the principle of least privilege.* | NCR |

**ASSESSMENT METHODS AND CANDIDATE ARTIFACTS FOR REVIEW**
Examine: [*SELECT FROM:* Access control policy; procedures addressing account management;  system security plan; system design documentation; system configuration settings and associated documentation; list of active system accounts and the name of the individual associated with each account; list of conditions for group and role membership; notifications or records of recently transferred, separated, or terminated employees; list of recently disabled system accounts along with the name of the individual associated with each account; access authorization records; account management compliance reviews; system monitoring/audit records; procedures addressing least privilege; list of security functions (deployed in hardware, software, and firmware) and security-relevant information for which access is to be explicitly authorized; list of system-generated privileged accounts; list of system administration personnel; other relevant documents or records].

Test: [*SELECT FROM:* Organizational processes for managing system accounts; mechanisms for implementing account management; mechanisms implementing least privilege functions; mechanisms prohibiting privileged access to the system].

## 3.1.6 Use non-privileged accounts or roles when accessing nonsecurity functions.

MINIMUM ANSWER: It is best to always first answer controls from a policy or procedural solution.  Essentially, this is preventing "general users" from accessing the C/U infrastructure and creating accounts, deleting databases, or elevating their privileges to gain access to both

CUI/CDI and sensitive C/U data. This is about providing the least amount of access and privilege based upon the duties assigned. Companies will see the control below that mandates a separation not just of duties, but access as well based on position and a clear need-to-know.

MORE COMPLETE ANSWER: The more-complete answer could be through automated solutions that monitor access of other security functions such as password resets, account creation, etc. This could include logging and review of all system access. It could also include automated tools that restrict access based upon a user's rights. These technical settings within the tool are established by C/U policy and monitored by, for example, the local SA.

| ASSESSMENT OBJECTIVE *Determine if:* | | |
|---|---|---|
| **SUB-CTRL** | *DESCRIPTION* | **RECOMMENDED APPROACH** |
| **3.1.6[a]** | *Nonsecurity functions are identified.* | NCR |
| **3.1.6[b]** | *Users are required to use non-privileged accounts or roles when accessing nonsecurity functions.* | P-This statement should be part of the C/U policy: *"Users are required to use non-privileged accounts or roles when accessing nonsecurity functions." (Best way to ensure completeness).* |

POTENTIAL ASSESSMENT METHODS AND CANDIDATE ARTIFACTS FOR REVIEW
Examine: [SELECT FROM: Access control policy; procedures addressing least privilege; system security plan; list of system-generated security functions assigned to system accounts or roles; system configuration settings and associated documentation; system audit logs and records; other relevant documents or records].
Test: [SELECT FROM: Mechanisms implementing least privilege functions].

## 3.1.7 Prevent non-privileged users from executing privileged functions and audit the execution of such functions.

MINIMUM ANSWER: There are many apparent similarities of the controls, and that was originally designed into NIST 800-171 for a reason. Security controls are supposed to be reinforcing, and this control is only slightly different in its scope than others described earlier.

Control 3.1.6 is similar is reinforcing this control as well as others. The C/U 's procedure guide can explicitly "rewrite" the original control description: "Prevent non-privileged users from executing privileged functions...." An example procedure write-up based upon the original control description is provided:

EXAMPLE PROCEDURE: *Non-privileged users are prohibited from executing any privileged functions or system audits without the authority of the C/U 's Chief Operating Officer, Chief Information Security Officer, or their designated representative. All requests will be submitted in writing with their first-line supervisor validating the need for such access for a limited and specified time.*

Additionally, this procedure limits higher-order (privileged) functions such as creating accounts for others, deleting database files, etc. It also requires the auditing of all privileged functions. It is suggested that the assigned SA at least weekly review and report inconsistencies of non-privileged/general users attempting (and, hopefully failing) to access parts of the internal infrastructure.

MORE COMPLETE ANSWER: A more thorough representation would be to provide copies of audit logs that include who, when, and what were the results of an audit evaluation; these artifacts should demonstrate that the C/U is following its internal cybersecurity procedures.

NOTE ABOUT "FREQUENCY": Many of the controls do not define how often a C/U should conduct a review, reassessment, etc. The C/U is afforded the opportunity to "define success" to the government Contract Officer or cybersecurity assessor. The important consideration is that the C/U determines the frequency of reviews, in general, based upon the perceived or actual sensitivity of the data. This book will typically provide the more stringent government frequency standard, but nothing prevents a C/U from conducting less often reviews if it can be substantiated.

| ASSESSMENT OBJECTIVE *Determine if:* | | |
|---|---|---|
| **SUB-CTRL** | *DESCRIPTION* | **RECOMMENDED APPROACH** |
| **3.1.7[a]** | *Privileged functions are defined.* | NCR |
| **3.1.7[b]** | *Non-privileged users are defined.* | NCR |
| **3.1.7[c]** | *Non-privileged users are prevented from executing privileged functions.* | NCR |
| **3.1.7[d]** | *The execution of privileged functions is captured in audit logs.* | P- Example policy statement update might read as: *"privileged functions are always captured and reviewed within audit logs weekly."* |

**POTENTIAL ASSESSMENT METHODS AND CANDIDATE ARTIFACTS FOR REVIEW**

Examine: [*SELECT FROM:* Access control policy; procedures addressing least privilege; system security plan; system design documentation; list of privileged functions and associated user account assignments; system configuration settings and associated documentation; system audit logs and records; other relevant documents or records].

Test: [*SELECT FROM:* Mechanisms implementing least privilege functions for non-privileged users; mechanisms auditing the execution of privileged functions].

### 3.1.8 Limit unsuccessful logon attempts.

MINIMUM ANSWER:  Government standard policy is after three failed logins the system will automatically lock out the individual.  Suggest this should be no more than five failed logins especially if employees are not computer savvy.  This requires both the technical solution by the C/U  IT system and described in the C/U procedure guide.

MORE COMPLETE ANSWER: For example, the additional ability to provide a screen capture that provides an artifact showing what happens when an employee reaches the maximum number of logons would meet this control; this could be added to the submission packet.  It is also important to document procedures to include the process to regain network access.

| ASSESSMENT OBJECTIVE *Determine if:* | | |
|---|---|---|
| **SUB-CTRL** | *DESCRIPTION* | **RECOMMENDED APPROACH** |
| **3.1.8[a]** | *The means of limiting unsuccessful logon attempts is defined.* | T-This is looking for what is monitoring unsuccessful logons.  It could be as basic as: "The XYZ Operating System enforces failed logon attempts after 3 fails." |
| **3.1.8[b]** | *The defined means of limiting unsuccessful logon attempts is implemented.* | T- (See above) |
| **POTENTIAL ASSESSMENT METHODS AND CANDIDATE ARTIFACTS FOR REVIEW**<br>Examine: [*SELECT FROM:* Access control policy; procedures addressing unsuccessful logon attempts; system security plan; system design documentation; system configuration settings and associated documentation; system audit logs and records; other relevant documents or records].<br>Test: [*SELECT FROM:* Mechanisms implementing access control policy for unsuccessful logon attempts]. | | |

### 3.1.9 Provide privacy and security notices consistent with applicable CUI rules.

MINIMUM ANSWER: Provided below is a current version of a **Warning Banner** designed for C/U purposes.  It should either be physically posted on or near each terminal or on the on-screen logon (preferred); this should also always include consent to monitoring.  Recommend consulting with a legal representative for final approval and dissemination to employees.

# [C/U] Warning Banner

*Use of this or any other [C/U name] computer system constitutes consent to monitoring at all times.*

*This is a [C/U name] computer system. All [C/U name] computer systems and related equipment are intended for the communication, transmission, processing, and storage of official or other authorized information only. All [C/U name] computer systems are subject to monitoring at all times to ensure proper functioning of equipment and systems including security devices and systems, to prevent unauthorized use and violations of statutes and security regulations, to deter criminal activity, and for other similar purposes. Any user of a [C/U name] computer system should be aware that any information placed in the system is subject to monitoring and is not subject to any expectation of privacy.*

*If monitoring of this or any other [C/U name] computer system reveals possible evidence of the violation of criminal statutes, this evidence and any other related information, including identification information about the user, may be provided to law enforcement officials. If monitoring of this or any other [C/U name] computer systems reveals violations of security regulations or unauthorized use, employees who violate security regulations or make unauthorized use of [C/U name] computer systems are subject to appropriate disciplinary action.*

*Use of this or any other [C/U name] computer system constitutes consent to monitoring at all times.*

MORE COMPLETE ANSWER: Another consideration should be this policy also be coordinated with Human Resources (HR).  This could further include that all employees sign a copy of this notice, and it is placed in their official file.  Select and redacted copies could be used to demonstrate an active adherence to this requirement as a sampling provided to the government.  It could also potentially describe how the C/U can take actions against personnel who fail or violate this warning.

| ASSESSMENT OBJECTIVE *Determine if:* | | |
|---|---|---|
| **SUB-CTRL** | **DESCRIPTION** | **RECOMMENDED APPROACH** |
| 3.1.9[a] | *Privacy and security notices required by CUI-specified rules are identified, consistent, and associated with the specific CUI category.* | NCR |

| 3.1.9[b] | *Privacy and security notices are displayed.* | NCR (This can be either physically displayed or when logging in [preferred]). |
|---|---|---|

**POTENTIAL ASSESSMENT METHODS AND CANDIDATE ARTIFACTS FOR REVIEW**

Examine: [*SELECT FROM:* Privacy and security policies, procedures addressing system use notification; documented approval of system use notification messages or banners; system audit logs and records; system design documentation; user acknowledgements of notification message or banner; system security plan; system use notification messages; system configuration settings and associated documentation; other relevant documents or records].

Test: [*SELECT FROM:* Mechanisms implementing system use notification].

## 3.1.10. Use session lock with pattern-hiding displays to prevent access/viewing of data after a period of inactivity.

MINIMUM ANSWER: While this may appear as solely a technical solution, it too should be identified in the C/U policy or procedure document.  Session lock describes the period of inactivity when a computer terminal will automatically lock out the user.  Suggest no more than 10 minutes for a computer lockout. Selecting longer is acceptable based upon many factors such as the type of work done (e.g., finance personnel) or the physical security level of the C/U (e.g., a restricted area with a limited number of authorized employees) is acceptable.  However, be prepared to defend the balance between the C/U 's need to meet government mission requirements and the risks of excessive session lock timeouts.

Secondarily, **Pattern Hiding** is desired to prevent the concept of "shoulder surfing."  Other like terms that are synonymous include **masking** and **obfuscation**.

Pattern hiding is designed to prevent an individual from observing an employee typing their password or Personal Identification Number (PIN). This control could include asterisks (*), for example, that mask the true information.  This prevents insiders or even visitors from "stealing" another user's login credentials.

Password without Pattern Hiding: PA$$w0rD

Password with Pattern Hiding:  ********

**Pattern Hiding**

---

MORE COMPLETE ANSWER: The better solution could include much shorter periods for a time-out, and longer password length and complexity; the standard is at least 15 alpha-numeric and special characters.

- Alpha: abcde....
- Numeric: 12345...
- Special Characters: @ # $ % ....

(See Control 3.13.10 for a further discussion of **Multifactor Authentication (MFA)** and **Two Factor Authentication (2FA)).**

As an ongoing reminder, it is critical to place artifacts describing the technical solution demonstrated, for example, using screen capture. It should be clear and easily traceable to this control's implementation by an audit representative or assessor.

| ASSESSMENT OBJECTIVE *Determine if:* | | |
|---|---|---|
| **SUB-CTRL** | *DESCRIPTION* | **RECOMMENDED APPROACH** |
| **3.1.10[a]** | *The period of inactivity after which the system initiates a session lock is defined.* | NCR |
| **3.1.10[b]** | *Access to the system and viewing of data is prevented by initiating a session lock after the defined period of inactivity.* | NCR |
| **3.1.10[c]** | *Previously visible information is concealed via a pattern-hiding display after the defined period of inactivity.* | NCR |
| **POTENTIAL ASSESSMENT METHODS AND CANDIDATE ARTIFACTS FOR REVIEW** Examine: [*SELECT FROM:* Access control policy; procedures addressing session lock; procedures addressing identification and authentication; system design documentation; system configuration settings and associated documentation; system security plan; other relevant documents or records]. Test: [*SELECT FROM:* Mechanisms implementing access control policy for session lock]. | | |

## 3.1.11. Terminate (automatically) a user session after a defined condition.

MINIMUM ANSWER: The simplest solution is a setting that the SA or other designated IT personnel, sets within the network's operating and management applications. Typically, most network operating systems can be set to enforce a terminal/complete lockout. This control implementation completely logs out the user and terminates any communications' sessions to include, for example, access to C/U databases, financial systems, or the Internet. It requires employees to re-initiate session connections to the network after this more-complete session logout occurs.

MORE COMPLETE ANSWER: The complete answer could include screen captures of policy settings for session terminations and time-outs. The SA or designated C/U representative should be able to provide as an artifact.

| ASSESSMENT OBJECTIVE *Determine if:* | | |
|---|---|---|
| **SUB-CTRL** | **DESCRIPTION** | **RECOMMENDED APPROACH** |
| 3.1.11[a] | *Conditions requiring a user session to terminate are defined.* | NCR |
| 3.1.11[b] | *A user session is automatically terminated after any of the defined conditions occur.* | NCR |

**POTENTIAL ASSESSMENT METHODS AND CANDIDATE ARTIFACTS FOR REVIEW**

Examine: [*SELECT FROM:* Access control policy; procedures addressing session termination; system design documentation; system security plan; system configuration settings and associated documentation; list of conditions or trigger events requiring session disconnect; system audit logs and records; other relevant documents or records].

Test: [*SELECT FROM:* Mechanisms implementing user session termination].

## 3.1.12 Monitor and control remote access sessions.

MINIMUM ANSWER: This control is about remote access where one computer can control another computer over the Internet.  This may include desktop support personnel "remoting into" an employee's computer to update the latest version of Firefox ® or a work-at-home employee inputting financial data into the C/U finance system.  Identify these types of access as part of the procedural guide and describe who is authorized, how their access is limited (such as a finance employee can't issue themselves a C/U check), and the repercussions of violating the policy.

MORE COMPLETE ANSWER: The better technological approach could include restrictions to only IT help personnel using remote capabilities. C/U policy should require regular review of auditable events and logs.  A screen capture would be helpful to show the policy settings specific to the remote desktop application.

| ASSESSMENT OBJECTIVE *Determine if:* | | |
|---|---|---|
| **SUB-CTRL** | **DESCRIPTION** | **RECOMMENDED APPROACH** |
| 3.1.12[a] | *Remote access sessions are permitted.* | P-Only for authorized personnel with a clear need |
| 3.1.12[b] | *The types of permitted remote access are identified.* | NCR |
| 3.1.12[c] | *Remote access sessions are controlled.* | NCR |
| 3.1.12[d] | *Remote access sessions are monitored.* | P-Recommend that these sessions be logged for all users. |

## 3.1.13 Employ cryptographic mechanisms to protect the confidentiality of remote access sessions.

MINIMUM ANSWER: ***This is a Data in Transit (DIT) issue***. Ensure the procedure requires the C/U 's solution only uses approved cryptographic solutions. The **Advanced Encryption Standard** (AES) is considered the current standard for encryption within the federal government. Also, use the 256 kilobyte (kb) key length versions.

There are many commercial solutions in this area. Major software companies provide solutions that secure DIT and are typically at reasonable prices for small C/U options such as Symantec ®, McAfee ®, and Microsoft®.

## ---*Again, document, document, document*

MORE COMPLETE ANSWER: (See Control 3.1.3 for a more detailed representation). It's usually a capability directly afforded by the remote access application tool providers. The more critical issue within the government is whether the application tool C/U ensure the application is coming from a US-based software developer.

There are many overseas developers, for example, to include Russia, former Warsaw Pact countries, and China, that are of concern to the US government. The apprehension is about commercial products from these nations and their potential threat to US national security. The C/U should confirm the product is coming from a current ally of the US; these would include the United Kingdom, Australia, etc. ***Before purchasing, ensure you have done your homework, and provide proof the remote access software is accepted by the federal government.***

| ASSESSMENT OBJECTIVE *Determine if:* | | |
|---|---|---|
| **SUB-CTRL** | *DESCRIPTION* | **RECOMMENDED APPROACH** |
| **3.1.13[a]** | *Cryptographic mechanisms to protect the confidentiality of remote access sessions are identified.* | NCR |
| **3.1.13[b]** | *Cryptographic mechanisms to protect the confidentiality of remote access sessions are implemented.* | NCR |

## 3.1.14 Route remote access via managed access control points.

MINIMUM ANSWER: **Managed access control** points are about control of traffic through "trusted" connections. For example, this could be Verizon ® or AT&T® as the C/U 's Internet Service Provider (ISP). It would be highly recommended to include any contracted services or Service Level Agreements (SLA) from these providers. They may include additional threat and spam filtering services that could reduce the "bad guys" from gaining access to C/U data; these are ideal artifacts for proof of satisfactorily meeting this control.

MORE COMPLETE ANSWER: Another addition could also be using what is called a **Virtual Private Network (VPN).** These are also common services the major providers have for additional costs.

Describing and providing such agreements could also identify a **defense in depth** approach; the first level is through the VPN service, and the second would be provided by the remote access software providing an additional layer of defense. Defense in depth can include such protective efforts to prevent unauthorized access to C/U IT assets:

- Physical protection (e.g., alarms, guards)
- Perimeter (e.g., firewalls, Intrusion Detection System (IDS), "Trusted Internet Connections")
- Application/Executables (e.g., **whitelisting** of authorized software, **blacklisting** blocking specified programs)
- Data (e.g., Data Loss Protection programs, Access controls, auditing)

| ASSESSMENT OBJECTIVE *Determine if:* | | |
|---|---|---|
| **SUB-CTRL** | *DESCRIPTION* | **RECOMMENDED APPROACH** |
| **3.1.14[a]** | *Managed access control points are identified and implemented.* | NCR |
| **3.1.14[b]** | *Remote access is routed through managed network access control points.* | NCR |

## 3.1.15 Authorize remote execution of privileged commands and remote access to security-relevant information.

MINIMUM ANSWER:  NIST 800-53 is the base document for all controls of NIST 800-171. It describes what C/U should manage and authorize privileged access to **security-relevant** information (e.g., finance information, IP, etc.), and using remote access only for "compelling operational needs."

This would specifically be documented in the restrictions of who and under what circumstances security-relevant information may be accessed by C/U personnel.  The base NIST control requires the C/U to document the rationale for this access in the System Security Plan (SSP); the interpretation is that the C/U cybersecurity policy should be an annex or appendix to the **SSP**. (See *System Security Plan (SSP) Template and Workbook"* on Amazon®)

MORE COMPLETE ANSWER: The ideal artifact suggested are the logs of remote access within and external to the C/U.  This could also be found in the firewall audit logs as well as the remote access software application logs for comparison; these could also be used to identify log modifications that may be an indicator of **insider threat**. (See Control 3.2.3 for further discussion of this topic area).

| ASSESSMENT OBJECTIVE *Determine if:* | | |
|---|---|---|
| **SUB-CTRL** | *DESCRIPTION* | **RECOMMENDED APPROACH** |
| **3.1.15[a]** | *Privileged commands authorized for remote execution are identified.* | P-Updates to policy should identify those "commands" that could compromise data such as changing prices, for example, without a requisite second party review, i.e., "separation of duties." |
| **3.1.15[b]** | *Security-relevant information authorized to be accessed remotely is identified.* | NCR |
| **3.1.15[c]** | *The execution of the identified privileged commands via remote access is authorized.* | NCR |
| **3.1.15[d]** | *Access to the identified security-relevant information via remote access is authorized.* | NCR |

**ASSESSMENT METHODS AND CANDIDATE ARTIFACTS FOR REVIEW**
Examine: [*SELECT FROM:* Access control policy; procedures addressing remote access to the system; system configuration settings and associated documentation; system security plan; system audit logs and records; other relevant documents or records].
Test: [*SELECT FROM:* Mechanisms implementing remote access management].

## 3.1.16 Authorize wireless access prior to allowing such connections.

MINIMUM ANSWER: This would include wireless access agreements and more commonly described earlier is an Acceptable Use Policy (AUP). For example, an AUP would include defining the types and kinds of sites restricted from access by employees. These are typically gambling, pornography sites, etc. AUP's should be reviewed by a lawyer before requiring employees to sign.

MORE COMPLETE ANSWER: The more-complete technical solution could identify unapproved sites and prevent "guest" access. (While guest access is not recommended, it is better to establish a secondary Wi-Fi network to accommodate and restrict visitors and third-party personnel from having direct access to the C/U network.)

It is also important that the Wi-Fi's network topology and encryption standard be provided as an artifact to the government once the final packet is ready for submission. This should be part of the SSP and the C/U cybersecurity procedure document.

| ASSESSMENT OBJECTIVE *Determine if:* | | |
| --- | --- | --- |
| **SUB-CTRL** | *DESCRIPTION* | **RECOMMENDED APPROACH** |
| **3.1.16[a]** | *Wireless access points are identified.* | NCR (Specifically, part of the SSP) |
| **3.1.16[b]** | *Wireless access is authorized prior to allowing such connections.* | NCR |

**POTENTIAL ASSESSMENT METHODS AND CANDIDATE ARTIFACTS FOR REVIEW**

Examine: [*SELECT FROM:* Access control policy; configuration management plan; procedures addressing wireless access implementation and usage (including restrictions); system security plan; system design documentation; system configuration settings and associated documentation; wireless access authorizations; system audit logs and records; other relevant documents or records].

Test: [*SELECT FROM:* Wireless access management capability for the system].

## 3.1.17 Protect wireless access using authentication and encryption.

MINIMUM ANSWER: Ensure this is included in the C/U procedure or policy that only authorized personnel within the firm to have access and that the appropriate level of encryption is in place. Currently, the 802.11 standard is used and Wi-Fi Protected Access 2 (WPA2) encryption should be the minimum standard.

MORE COMPLETE ANSWER: Use of Wi-Fi "sniffing technology" while available may be prohibitively costly to smaller C/Us. This technology can identify and audit unauthorized entry into the wireless portion of the network and subsequently provides access to the "physical" C/U network. Sniffers can be used to notify security personnel either through email or Short Message Service (SMS)-text alerts of such intrusions; if C/U data is highly sensitive, then this investment may be necessary. Also, maintain any documentation about the "sniffer" and its capabilities; provide it to government representatives as part of the official submission.

| ASSESSMENT OBJECTIVE *Determine if:* | | |
|---|---|---|
| **SUB-CTRL** | *DESCRIPTION* | **RECOMMENDED APPROACH** |
| **3.1.17[a]** | *Wireless access to the system is protected using authentication.* | NCR |
| **3.1.17[b]** | *Wireless access to the system is protected using encryption.* | NCR |

**ASSESSMENT METHODS AND CANDIDATE ARTIFACTS FOR REVIEW**

Examine: [*SELECT FROM:* Access control policy; system design documentation; procedures addressing wireless implementation and usage (including restrictions); system security plan; system configuration settings and associated documentation; system audit logs and records; other relevant documents or records].

Test: [*SELECT FROM:* Mechanisms implementing wireless access protections to the system].

## 3.1.18. Control connection of mobile devices.

MINIMUM ANSWER: Most C/U's mobile devices are their cell phones. This would also include laptops and computer "pads" with web-enabled capabilities. This would first require as a matter of policy that employees only use secure connections for their devices when not using the C/U 's service provider—these should be verified as secure. This would also specifically bar employees use of unsecured Wi-fi **hot spots** such as fast food restaurants, coffee shops, etc. Home Wi-fi networks are typically secure but ensure that employees know to select **WPA2** as their standard at-home secure connection protocol.

MORE COMPLETE ANSWER: A better way to demonstrate this control is by discussing with the cell phone provider the ability to prevent C/U phones from using unsecure Wi-Fi networks at any time. The provider should be able to block access if the mobile phone does not "see" or recognize a secure connection. Include any proof from service agreements of such a provision as part of the submitted BOE.

| ASSESSMENT OBJECTIVE *Determine if:* | | |
|---|---|---|
| **SUB-CTRL** | *DESCRIPTION* | **RECOMMENDED APPROACH** |
| **3.1.18[a]** | *Mobile devices that process, store, or transmit CUI are identified.* | P-Ensure an artifact is updated with carriers at least monthly (recommended) |
| **3.1.18[b]** | *Mobile device connections are authorized.* | NCR |
| **3.1.18[c]** | *Mobile device connections are monitored and logged.* | P/T-Policy and notification to users should be documented and signed by |

| | | every user (e.g., the AUP) and the carrier provides logs as requested or required. |
|---|---|---|

**ASSESSMENT METHODS AND CANDIDATE ARTIFACTS FOR REVIEW**

Examine: [*SELECT FROM:* Access control policy; authorizations for mobile device connections to organizational systems; procedures addressing access control for mobile device usage (including restrictions); system design documentation; configuration management plan; system security plan; system audit logs and records; system configuration settings and associated documentation; other relevant documents or records].

Test: [*SELECT FROM:* Access control capability authorizing mobile device connections to organizational systems].

## 3.1.19. Encrypt CUI on mobile devices.

MINIMUM ANSWER: The good news is that all the major carriers provide DAR encryption. Mobile phones typically can secure DAR on the phone behind a passcode, PIN, or even biometric capability such as fingerprint or facial recognition; these are acceptable by government standards. Check service agreements or add to the C/U 's existing plan.

MORE COMPLETE ANSWER: There are several companies that provide proprietary and hardened devices for C/U users. These include state of the art encryption standards and further hardened phone bodies to prevent physical exploits of lost or stolen mobile devices. *Expect these solutions to be very expensive.*

**ASSESSMENT OBJECTIVE** *Determine if:*

| SUB-CTRL | DESCRIPTION | RECOMMENDED APPROACH |
|---|---|---|
| 3.1.19[a] | *Mobile devices and mobile computing platforms that process, store, or transmit CUI are identified.* | NCR |
| 3.1.19[b] | *Encryption is employed to protect CUI on identified mobile devices and mobile computing platforms.* | NCR |

**ASSESSMENT METHODS AND CANDIDATE ARTIFACTS FOR REVIEW**

Examine: [*SELECT FROM:* Access control policy; procedures addressing access control for mobile devices; system design documentation; system configuration settings and associated documentation; encryption mechanisms and associated configuration documentation; system security plan; system audit logs and records; other relevant documents or records].

Test: [*SELECT FROM:* Encryption mechanisms protecting confidentiality of information on mobile devices].

## 3.1.20 Verify and control/limit connections to and use of external systems.

MINIMUM ANSWER: This control requires that all external or third-party connections to the C/U 's network be verified. This would typically take the form of accepting another C/U (or even federal agencies') Authority to Operate (ATO). This could be as simple as a memorandum, for example, recognizing another C/U 's self-assessment under NIST 800-171. It could also be accepted through a process known as **reciprocity**, of accepting an ATO based upon NIST 800-53—more typical of federal agencies. These are all legitimate means that are designed to ensure before a C/U allows another C/U to enter through its firewall (system security boundary) without some level of certainty that security was fully considered. Before an external system or network is allowed unfettered access to the C/U s' data, it is critical to identify the rules and restrictions for such access as part of this control.

As always, ensure procedures identify, and limit, such connections to only critical data feeds needed from third-parties to conduct formal C/U operations.

MORE COMPLETE ANSWER: This could include a request for ongoing scans of the external system and/or network every 30 days; this would be considered quite extreme, but dependent on data sensitivity. If sought, suggest that every six-month that the C/U receives copies of the anti-virus, anti-malware, and vulnerability patch scanning reports to identify current threats to the external system. This is designed to address inbound threats potentially and to enhance the C/U 's overall security posture.

| ASSESSMENT OBJECTIVE *Determine if:* | | |
|---|---|---|
| **SUB-CTRL** | *DESCRIPTION* | **RECOMMENDED APPROACH** |
| **3.1.20[a]** | *Connections to external systems are identified.* | SSP-Should be identified in architecture diagram |
| **3.1.20[b]** | *The use of external systems is identified.* | SSP- (See above) |
| **3.1.20[c]** | *Connections to external systems are verified.* | NCR |
| **3.1.20[d]** | *The use of external systems is verified.* | NCR |
| **3.1.20[e]** | *Connections to external systems are controlled/limited.* | NCR |
| **3.1.20[f]** | *The use of external systems is controlled/limited.* | NCR |

**ASSESSMENT METHODS AND CANDIDATE ARTIFACTS FOR REVIEW**

Examine: [*SELECT FROM:* Access control policy; procedures addressing the use of external systems; terms and conditions for external systems; system security plan; list of applications accessible from external systems; system configuration settings and associated documentation; system connection or processing agreements; account management documents; other relevant documents or records].

Test: [*SELECT FROM:* Mechanisms implementing terms and conditions on use of external systems].

## 3.1.21 Limit use of organizational portable storage devices on external systems.

MINIMUM ANSWER: This is not only about the use of USB thumb drives (see Chapter on Media Protection (MP)), it is also about external drives attached to a workstation or laptop, locally.

While thumb drives are more capable of introducing malware and viruses to an unprotected network, external drives pose a real threat to data removal and theft. The C/U policy should include an approval process to "attach" only C/U provided drives and highly discourage personal devices attached by employees. Technical support should include the active scanning for viruses and malware every time the portable device is attached to the network.

MORE COMPLETE ANSWER: As discussed in more detail below regarding the use of thumb drives, IT personnel could disable anyone from using the **registry**. Where the need for external drives is necessitated, this control can be further enhanced through auditing of all such attachments and provide pre-formatted reports for C/U leadership. Auditing, as described under the AU control, should include capturing this activity.

| ASSESSMENT OBJECTIVE *Determine if:* | | |
|---|---|---|
| **SUB-CTRL** | *DESCRIPTION* | **RECOMMENDED APPROACH** |
| **3.1.21[a]** | *The use of portable storage devices containing CUI on external systems is identified and documented.* | NCR |
| **3.1.21[b]** | *Limits on the use of portable storage devices containing CUI on external systems are defined.* | NCR |
| **3.1.21[c]** | *The use of portable storage devices containing CUI on external systems is limited as defined.* | NCR |

**ASSESSMENT METHODS AND CANDIDATE ARTIFACTS FOR REVIEW**

Examine: [*SELECT FROM*: Access control policy; procedures addressing the use of external systems; system security plan; system configuration settings and associated documentation; system connection or processing agreements; account management documents; other relevant documents or records].

Test: [*SELECT FROM*: Mechanisms implementing restrictions on use of portable storage devices].

## 3.1.22 Control CUI posted or processed on publicly accessible systems.

MINIMUM ANSWER: This addresses the control of publicly accessible information most commonly on the C/U 's **public-facing** website. There needs to be procedural guidance and direction about who can release (usually public affairs office, etc.) and post information (usually webmaster, etc.) to the website. This should include a review of such data by personnel specifically trained to recognize CUI/CDI data. This may include information or data that discusses a C/U 's current C/U relationship with the government, the activities it conducts, and the products and services it provides to both the public and private sector.

This should also address the regular review of publicly accessible data, and the procedure to describe the process to remove unauthorized data if discovered.

MORE COMPLETE ANSWER: This could use automated scans of keywords and phrases that may alert audit personnel during their regular auditing activities. See the Auditing Control (AU) chapter. While this is a static means to alert untrained IT personnel, it could supplement that inadvertent release does not occur. Additional oversight should always be based upon the sensitivity of the information handled to not only include CUI/CDI, but Intellectual Property (IP) or other sensitive data, etc., that may harm the C/U if released into the public.

| ASSESSMENT OBJECTIVE *Determine if:* | | |
|---|---|---|
| **SUB-CTRL** | *DESCRIPTION* | **RECOMMENDED APPROACH** |
| **3.1.22[a]** | *Individuals authorized to post or process information on publicly accessible systems are identified.* | NCR |
| **3.1.22[b]** | *Procedures to ensure CUI is not posted or processed on publicly accessible systems are identified.* | NCR |
| **3.1.22[c]** | *A review process is in place prior to posting of any content to publicly accessible systems.* | NCR |
| **3.1.22[d]** | *Content on publicly accessible systems is reviewed to ensure that it does not include CUI.* | NCR |
| **3.1.22[e]** | *Mechanisms are in place to remove and address improper posting of CUI.* | NCR |

ASSESSMENT METHODS AND CANDIDATE ARTIFACTS FOR REVIEW
Examine: [SELECT FROM: Access control policy; procedures addressing publicly accessible content; system security plan; list of users authorized to post publicly accessible content on organizational systems; training materials and/or records; records of publicly accessible information reviews; records of response to nonpublic information on public websites; system audit logs and records; security awareness training records; other relevant documents or records].
Test: [SELECT FROM: Mechanisms implementing management of publicly accessible content].

*The decision process of how much encryption and added protection (such as hashing or emerging blockchain encryption technologies) should be based on the risk to the system.*

*Consider the risk and the damage to the C/U if the data, CUI or not is compromised*

# AWARENESS & TRAINING (AT)

## A training program is a must

Awareness & Training is about an active cybersecurity training program for employees and a recurring education program that ensures their familiarity and compliance with protecting sensitive and CUI/CDI C/U data consistently. The websites (below) identify FREE government-sponsored sites a C/U can leverage without expending any of its own resources. The three major training requirements that can be expected of most vendors supporting federal government contract activities include:

1. **Cybersecurity Awareness Training.**
   https://securityawareness.usalearning.gov/cybersecurity/index.htm

2. **Insider Threat Training.**
   https://securityawareness.usalearning.gov/itawareness/index.htm
   (More discussion on the "Insider Threat" topic See Control 3.2.3).

3. **Privacy.**
   https://iatraining.disa.mil/eta/piiv2/launchPage.htm (This would specifically apply to any C/U that handles, processes or maintains Personally Identifiable Information (PII) and Personal Health Information (PHI). The author's expectation is that even though a C/U does not handle PII or PHI, the federal government to make this a universal training requirement.)

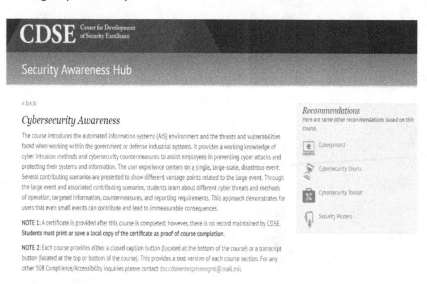

Defense Security Service (DSS) Cybersecurity Awareness Site

## Basic Security Requirements:

**3.2.1 Ensure that managers, systems administrators, and users of organizational information systems are made aware of the security risks associated with their activities and of the applicable policies, standards, and procedures related to the security of organizational information systems.**

MINIMUM ANSWER: Human beings are the weakest link in the cybersecurity "war." The greatest threat is from the employee who unwittingly selects a link that allows an intrusion into the C/U system, or worse, those who maliciously remove, modify, or delete sensitive CUI/CDI.

The answer should be documented regarding initial and annual refresher training requirements for everyone in the C/U; not average employees but must include senior managers and support subcontractors. Provide a sampling of select employees that have taken training, and ensuring it is current within the past year.

MORE COMPLETE ANSWER: A possible demonstration of the more-complete solution is within the policy specific direction to IT support personnel. There could be a system notification that allows them after notification, manually or by automated means, to suspend access to training is completed. Strong documentation is important specific to awareness training.

| ASSESSMENT OBJECTIVE *Determine if:* | | |
|---|---|---|
| **SUB-CTRL** | *DESCRIPTION* | **RECOMMENDED APPROACH** |
| **3.2.1[a]** | *Security risks associated with organizational activities involving CUI are identified.* | P-This would take the form of an initial and follow-on Risk Assessment (RA) for this control. Recommend an RA is conducted by the CIO, CISO, or like IT representative who conducts and review this review with senior leadership annually. |
| **3.2.1[b]** | *Policies, standards, and procedures related to the security of the system are identified.* | P- *"Policies, standards, and procedures related to the security of the system are identified AND DOCUMENTED annually in conjunction with a C/U RA [see above]."* |
| **3.2.1[c]** | *Managers, systems administrators, and users of the system are made aware of the security risks associated with their activities.* | P-Add to current and future updates to cybersecurity awareness training specific to an RA. |
| **3.2.1[d]** | *Managers, systems administrators, and users of the system are made aware of the applicable policies, standards, and procedures related to the security of the system.* | P-Add to current and future updates to cybersecurity awareness training specific to an RA. |

## 3.2.2 Ensure that organizational personnel are adequately trained to carry out their assigned information security-related duties and responsibilities.

MINIMUM ANSWER: This is required not only awareness training but also specialized training for privileged users.  This is usually Operating System (OS) training specific to the C/U 's architecture.  It is possible to have multiple OS's.  Privileged users are only required to show, for example, some form of the training certificate, to meet this requirement.  All IT personnel who have elevated privileges must have such training before they are authorized to execute their duties.

Additionally, if the C/U uses Microsoft ® or Linux ® Operating Systems, privileged users will have some level of certification to show a familiarity with these programs.  This could include major national certifications for these applications or basic familiarity courses from free training sites, for example, Khan Academy® (https://www.khanacademy.org/) or Udacity® (https://www.udacity.com/).

The government has not defined the level and type of training for this requirement.  It requires privileged users to have an understanding and training certificate (with no specified time length) for the major Operating System (OS) the C/U IT infrastructure employs.

MORE COMPLETE ANSWER: If IT personnel have formal certification (such as from a Microsoft ® partner training program), these are ideal artifacts that should be part of the BOE.

| ASSESSMENT OBJECTIVE *Determine if:* | | |
|---|---|---|
| **SUB-CTRL** | **DESCRIPTION** | **RECOMMENDED APPROACH** |
| **3.2.2[a]** | *Information security-related duties, roles, and responsibilities are defined.* | NCR |
| **3.2.2[b]** | *Information security-related duties, roles, and responsibilities are assigned to designated personnel.* | NCR |
| **3.2.2[c]** | *Personnel are adequately trained to carry out their assigned information security-related duties, roles, and responsibilities.* | NCR |

## Derived Security Requirements:

## 3.2.3 Provide security awareness training on recognizing and reporting potential indicators of insider threat.

MINIMUM ANSWER: The DOD's Defense Security Service (DSS) in Quantico, VA, is the executive agent for insider threat activities. The DSS provides many training opportunities and toolkits on Insider Threat.  These are available from their agency website for free at http://www.dss.mil/it/index.html.  This is an excellent resource to create an insider threat training program already developed for the C/U 's use.

Document C/U minimum training requirements for both general and privileged users such as watching select online instruction or computer-based training opportunities from DSS. Everyone in the C/U should participate and satisfactorily complete the training.

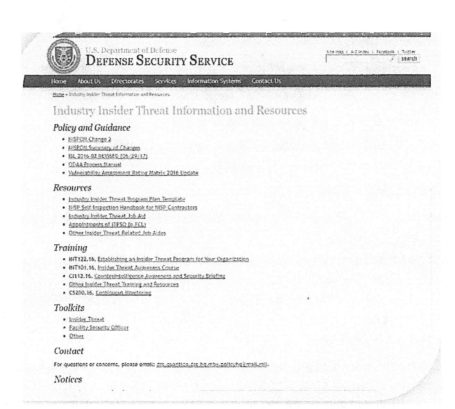

MORE COMPLETE ANSWER: More-complete proof of C/U compliance with this security control requirement might include guest speakers, or insider threat brown-bag events around lunch time. C/U training personnel should capture attendance records to include sign-in rosters. These could be used for annual training requirements specific to insider threat familiarity.

Also, recommend a **train-the-trainer program** where select individuals are trained by either DSS or other competent C/U that becomes C/U resources. These assigned individuals could provide both training and first-responder support as needed and be deployed to other C/U sites.

| ASSESSMENT OBJECTIVE *Determine if:* | | |
|---|---|---|
| **SUB-CTRL** | *DESCRIPTION* | **RECOMMENDED APPROACH** |
| **3.2.3[a]** | *Potential indicators associated with insider threats are identified.* | P-Identify this in association with a Risk Assessment (RA) as described in Control 3.2.2. |
| **3.2.3[b]** | *Security awareness training on recognizing and reporting potential indicators of insider threat is provided to managers and employees.* | NCR |

**ASSESSMENT METHODS AND CANDIDATE ARTIFACTS FOR REVIEW**

Examine: [*SELECT FROM:* Security awareness and training policy; procedures addressing security awareness training implementation; security awareness training curriculum; security awareness training materials; insider threat policy and procedures; system security plan; other relevant documents or records].

Test: [*SELECT FROM:* Mechanisms managing insider threat training].

# AUDIT AND ACCOUNTABILITY (AU)
## System Logs and their Regular Review

The AU control is primarily about the ability of the system owner/C/U to monitor unauthorized access to the system through system logging functions of the Operating System and other network devices such as firewalls. A SA is typically assigned the duty to review log files; these may include both authorized and unauthorized access to the network, applications, databases, financial systems, etc. Most C/U will rely on manual review; however, some "smart" servers and firewalls can provide automated alerts to IT personnel of unauthorized use or intrusion. The key is to understand the auditing capabilities of the C/U system and be prepared to defend its capabilities and limitations if government representatives or third-party assessors request proof of control compliance.

```
 ∟sion Detection System

.**]  [1:1407:9] SNMP trap udp [**]
[Classification: Attempted Information Leak] [Priority: 2]
03/06-8:14:09.082119 192.168.1.167:1052 -> 172.30.128.27:162
UDP TTL:118 TOS:0x0 ID:29101 IpLen:20 DgmLen:87


Personal Firewall

3/6/2006 8:14:07 AM,"Rule ""Block Windows File Sharing"" blocked (192.168.1.54,
netbios-ssn(139)).","Rule ""Block Windows File Sharing"" blocked (192.168.1.54,
netbios-ssn(139)).  Inbound TCP connection.  Local address,service is
(KENT(172.30.128.27),netbios-ssn(139)).  Remote address,service is
(192.168.1.54,39922).  Process name is ""System""."

3/3/2006 9:04:04 AM,Firewall configuration updated: 398 rules.,Firewall configuration
updated: 398 rules.


Antivirus Software, Log 1

3/4/2006 9:33:50 AM,Definition File Download,KENT,userk,Definition downloader
3/4/2006 9:33:09 AM,AntiVirus Startup,KENT,userk,System
3/3/2006 3:56:46 PM,AntiVirus Shutdown,KENT,userk,System


Antivirus Software, Log 2

240203071234,16,3,7,KENT,userk,,,,,,,16777216,"Virus definitions are
current.",0,,0,,,,,0,,,,,,,,,,SAVPROD,{ xxxxxxxx-xxxx-xxxx-xxxx-xxxxxxxxxxxx },End
User,(IP)-192.168.1.121,,GROUP,0:0:0:0:0:0,9.0.0.338,,,,,,,,,,,,,,


Antispyware Software

DSO Exploit: Data source object exploit (Registry change, nothing done)  HKEY_USERS\S-
1-5-19\Software\Microsoft\Windows\CurrentVersion\Internet Settings\Zones\0\1004!=W=³
```

**Audit log type examples.** The logs above are good examples of the system logs that should be reviewed regularly. These are the C/U 's responsibility to monitor the network actively. Another term of high interest is **Continuous Monitoring (ConMon);** see the article in Appendix C discussing the importance of ConMon capabilities. ConMon can be accomplished by both manual and automated means, and auditing is a major control family supporting the objectives of this cybersecurity principle.

ConMon activities are best described as the ability of the C/U to "continuously" monitor the state of its network within its defined security boundary. It should be a capability to determine, for example, who, when, and what are within the C/U 's security boundary and any reporting requirements in the event of an intrusion. It will be based on log discovery of unauthorized activities. (SOURCE: *Guide to Computer Security Log Management*, NIST SP 800-92, September 2006, http://nvlpubs.nist.gov/nistpubs/Legacy/SP/nistspecialpublication800-92.pdf) .

For a better description about the purpose and components of Continuous Monitoring (ConMon) see Appendix D: ***Continuous Monitoring: A More Detailed Discussion.***

---

**Basic Security Requirements:**

---

**3.3.1 Create, protect, and retain information system audit records to the extent needed to enable the monitoring, analysis, investigation, and reporting of unlawful, unauthorized, or inappropriate information system activity.**

MINIMUM ANSWER: The key part of this control is about audit record retention.  The control defines the retention period as a vague capability to retain such records to the greatest "extent possible."  The guidance should always be based on the sensitivity of the data.  Another consideration should include the ability to provide forensic data to investigators to determine the intrusion over a period.

The historical OPM Breach occurred over several years until OPM even recognized multiple incidents.  This included the exfiltration of millions of personnel and security background investigation files.  OPM failures while many, including poor audit processes and review, are a major factor in the success of nation-state hackers. OPM's poor audit and retention processes made reconstructing critical events more than difficult for government forensics and associated criminal investigations.

---

The recommendation to small and medium C/U conducting US government contract activities would be at least one year and preferably two years of audit log retention.  Companies should regularly discuss with government contract representatives its specified requirements.  They should also visit the National Archives Record Agency (NARA) (www.nara.gov) for CUI/CDI data retention as part of an active audit program.

---

---

*C/Us should balance operations (and long-term costs) with security (the ability to reconstruct an intrusion, to support law enforcement)*

---

MORE COMPLETE ANSWER: A greater ability to recognize breaches (events and incidents) could include an additional internal process and assigned first-responders who would act upon these occurrences. This response team may have the additional specialized training to include the use of select network analysis support tools to include packet inspection training using tools such as Wireshark ® (https://www.wireshark.org/ ).

| ASSESSMENT OBJECTIVE *Determine if:* | | |
|---|---|---|
| **SUB-CTRL** | *DESCRIPTION* | **RECOMMENDED APPROACH** |
| **3.3.1[a]** | *Audit logs needed (i.e., event types to be logged) to enable the monitoring, analysis, investigation, and reporting of unlawful or unauthorized system activity are specified.* | NCR |
| **3.3.1[b]** | *The content of audit records needed to support monitoring, analysis, investigation, and reporting of unlawful or unauthorized system activity is defined.* | NCR |
| **3.3.1[c]** | *Audit records are created (generated).* | NCR |
| **3.3.1[d]** | *Audit records, once created, contain the defined content.* | P - ("Defined content" is too vague. This should at a minimum be the login ID [the person], date-time stamp, IP address, MAC address and all commands executed). |
| **3.3.1[e]** | *Retention requirements for audit records are defined.* | NCR – Refer to National Archives Record Agency (NARA) (www.nara.gov) for CUI/CDI data retention. |
| **3.3.1[f]** | *Audit records are retained as defined.* | NCR |

**ASSESSMENT METHODS AND CANDIDATE ARTIFACTS FOR REVIEW**

Examine: [*SELECT FROM:* Audit and accountability policy; procedures addressing auditable events; system security plan; system design documentation; system configuration settings and associated documentation; procedures addressing control of audit records; procedures addressing audit record generation; system audit logs and records; system auditable events; system incident reports; other relevant documents or records].

Test: [*SELECT FROM:* Mechanisms implementing system audit logging].

## 3.3.2 Ensure that the actions of individual information system users can be uniquely traced to those users, so they can be held accountable for their actions.

MINIMUM ANSWER: This is about that capture of individual users as they access the system. Access logs should include, for example, user identification information, timestamps of all access, databases or applications accessed, and some failed login attempts. This control is designed for potential forensic reconstruction for either internal policy violations or external threat intrusions. Any policy considerations should include at least weekly review, but any audit review periodicity should be based on the sensitivity and criticality of data to the C/U 's overall mission.

MORE COMPLETE ANSWER: A more complete means to address this control is using automated alerts to key IT and management personnel. This could include capabilities from existing "smart" firewalls, or more advanced solutions may include a **Security Information & Event Management** (SIEM) solution. These are more complicated and expensive solutions, but current developments employing modern Artificial Intelligence and Machine Learning technologies to more proactively identify threats is evolving rapidly; these solutions should be less expensive and easier to deploy within the next decade.

| ASSESSMENT OBJECTIVE *Determine if:* | | |
|---|---|---|
| **SUB-CTRL** | *DESCRIPTION* | **RECOMMENDED APPROACH** |
| **3.3.2[a]** | *The content of the audit records needed to support the ability to uniquely trace users to their actions is defined.* | NCR |
| **3.3.2[b]** | *Audit records, once created, contain the defined content.* | NCR |

**ASSESSMENT METHODS AND CANDIDATE ARTIFACTS FOR REVIEW**

Examine: [*SELECT FROM:* Audit and accountability policy; procedures addressing audit records and event types; system security plan; system design documentation; system configuration settings and associated documentation; procedures addressing audit record generation; procedures addressing audit review, analysis, and reporting; reports of audit findings; system audit logs and records; system events; system incident reports; other relevant documents or records].

Test: [*SELECT FROM:* Mechanisms implementing system audit logging].

**Derived Security Requirements:**

### 3.3.3 Review and update audited events.

MINIMUM ANSWER: This is a similar requirement to other AU controls above to regularly review audit logs. We recommend at least weekly reviews.

MORE COMPLETE ANSWER: To more completely address this control, IT personnel could categorize the log types being collected. These could include, for example, Operating System (OS) (network), application, firewall, database logs, etc.

| ASSESSMENT OBJECTIVE *Determine if:* | | |
|---|---|---|
| **SUB-CTRL** | *DESCRIPTION* | **RECOMMENDED APPROACH** |
| **3.3.3[a]** | *A process for determining when to review logged events is defined.* | NCR |

| 3.3.3[b] | *Event types being logged are reviewed in accordance with the defined review process.* | *P- "Event types" could include failed logons, file deletions, modifications or changes (especially in critical databases such HR or finance).* |
|---|---|---|
| 3.3.3[c] | *Event types being logged are updated based on the review.* | *P- (See Above)* |

**ASSESSMENT METHODS AND CANDIDATE ARTIFACTS FOR REVIEW**

Examine: [*SELECT FROM:* Audit and accountability policy; procedures addressing audit records and event types; system security plan; list of organization-defined event types to be logged; reviewed and updated records of logged event types; system audit logs and records; system incident reports; other relevant documents or records].

Test: [*SELECT FROM:* Mechanisms supporting review and update of logged event types].

## 3.3.4 Alert in the event of an audit process failure.

MINIMUM ANSWER:  This is an active ability developed within the C/U 's audit technology that can alert personnel of an audit failure.

This could include local alarms, flashing lights, SMS, and email alerts to key C/U personnel. This will require SA and IT personnel to set policy settings to be established as part of the normal checks in support of the overall audit function and control.  A description of the technical implementation and immediate actions to be taken by personnel should be identified.  This should include activation of the Incident Response (IR) Plan.

MORE COMPLETE ANSWER: Additional technical solutions could include supplementary systems to be monitored.  This could include the state of all audit-capable devices and functions.  This may also include a separate computer or a backup auditing server for the storage of logs not on the primary system; this would prevent intruders from deleting or changing logs to hide their presence in the network.

These solutions will ultimately add additional complexity and cost.  Ensure any solution is supportable both financially and technically by C/U decision-makers. While to have greater security is an overall desire of the NIST 800-171 implementation, it should be balanced with a practical and measurable value-added approach to adding any new technologies.  It should also be a further consideration that the incorporation of new technologies should address the impacts of added complexity and determining the ability of IT support personnel to maintain it.

| ASSESSMENT OBJECTIVE *Determine if:* | | |
|---|---|---|
| **SUB-CTRL** | *DESCRIPTION* | **RECOMMENDED APPROACH** |
| **3.3.4[a]** | *Personnel or roles to be alerted in the event of an audit logging process failure are identified.* | NCR |
| **3.3.4[b]** | *Types of audit logging process failures for which alert will be generated are defined.* | NCR |
| **3.3.4[c]** | *Identified personnel or roles are alerted in the event of an audit logging process failure.* | NCR |

**ASSESSMENT METHODS AND CANDIDATE ARTIFACTS FOR REVIEW**

Examine: [*SELECT FROM:* Audit and accountability policy; procedures addressing response to audit logging processing failures; system design documentation; system security plan; system configuration settings and associated documentation; list of personnel to be notified in case of an audit logging processing failure; system incident reports; system audit logs and records; other relevant documents or records].

Test: [*SELECT FROM:* Mechanisms implementing system response to audit logging processing failures].

## 3.3.5 Correlate audit review, analysis, and reporting processes for investigation and response to indications of inappropriate, suspicious, or unusual activity.

MINIMUM ANSWER:  This should identify the technical actions taken by authorized audit personnel to pursue when analyzing suspicious activity on the network.

It should also be tied to the IR Plan, and be tested at least annually.  (See Control IR for further discussion of the **DOD Precedence Identification** example and determine actions based on the level of severity).

MORE COMPLETE ANSWER:  See Control 3.3.2 for a more detailed discussion of employing a SIEM solution. In addition to manual analysis, the C/U could leverage the capabilities of newer threat identification technologies such as SIEM and "smart" Intrusion Detection and Prevention devices.

| ASSESSMENT OBJECTIVE *Determine if:* | | |
|---|---|---|
| **SUB-CTRL** | *DESCRIPTION* | **RECOMMENDED APPROACH** |
| **3.3.5[a]** | *Audit record review, analysis, and reporting processes for investigation and response to indications of unlawful, unauthorized, suspicious, or unusual activity are defined.* | NCR |
| **3.3.5[b]** | *Defined audit record review, analysis, and reporting processes are correlated.* | NCR |

## 3.3.6 Provide audit reduction and report generation to support on-demand analysis and reporting.

MINIMUM ANSWER: Audit reduction provides for "on-demand" audit review, analysis, and reporting requirements.

This should at least use manual methods to collect audits from across multiple audit logging devices to assist with potential forensic needs. Any procedural effort to support audit reduction most likely can use commercial support applications and scripts (small programs typically are explicitly written to the C/U 's unique IT environment) that IT personnel should be able to assist in their identification, development, and procurement.

MORE COMPLETE ANSWER: IT personnel could identify more automated and integrated audit reduction solutions. Likely candidates could be "smart" firewalls or Security Information and Event Management (SIEM) solutions.

**ASSESSMENT OBJECTIVE** *Determine if:*

| SUB-CTRL | DESCRIPTION | RECOMMENDED APPROACH |
|---|---|---|
| 3.3.6[a] | *An audit record reduction capability that supports on-demand analysis is provided.* | NCR (if required to automate then a POAM or Waiver may be necessary) |
| 3.3.6[b] | *A report generation capability that supports on-demand reporting is provided.* | NCR (This could be as basic as a data-run to provide ad hoc reporting requests). |

## 3.3.7 Provide an information system capability that compares and synchronizes internal system clocks with an authoritative source to generate timestamps for audit records.

MINIMUM ANSWER: The simplest answer is to have IT personnel use the Network Time Protocol (NTP) on **NTP port 123** to provide US Naval Observatory timestamps as the standard for the network; this is considered the authoritative source. The system clocks of all processors (computers, firewalls, etc.) within the C/U should be set to the same time when first initialized by IT support staffs; this should be an explicit policy requirement.

It is suggested that SA personnel review and compare the external (NTP server time stamp) with internal system clocks. This can be used to identify log changes if synchronization is not the same from the external and internal clock settings. Log changes may be an indicator of unauthorized access and manipulation of log files by hackers.

MORE COMPLETE ANSWER:  There are several automated programs that can be used, and good basic programmers within the C/U could write scripts (small pieces of executable code) to provide these comparisons more easily.

| ASSESSMENT OBJECTIVE *Determine if:* | | |
|---|---|---|
| **SUB-CTRL** | *DESCRIPTION* | **RECOMMENDED APPROACH** |
| **3.3.7[a]** | *Internal system clocks are used to generate time stamps for audit records.* | P-The control here is calling for relying on "internal" clocks; BE AWARE hackers can manipulate system clocks. |
| **3.3.7[b]** | *An authoritative source with which to compare and synchronize internal system clocks is specified.* | NCR |
| **3.3.7[c]** | *Internal system clocks used to generate time stamps for audit records are compared to and synchronized with the specified authoritative time source.* | NCR |
| **POTENTIAL ASSESSMENT METHODS AND CANDIDATE ARTIFACTS FOR REVIEW**<br>Examine: [*SELECT FROM:* Audit and accountability policy; procedures addressing time stamp generation; system design documentation; system security plan; system configuration settings and associated documentation; system audit logs and records; other relevant documents or records].<br>Test: [*SELECT FROM:* Mechanisms implementing time stamp generation; mechanisms implementing internal information system clock synchronization]. | | |

## 3.3.8 Protect audit information and audit tools from unauthorized access, modification, and deletion.

MINIMUM ANSWER: This control requires greater protection of audit files and auditing tools from unauthorized users.  These tools can be exploited by intruders to change log files or delete them entirely to hide their entry into the system.  Password protect and limit use to only authorized personnel.  Document this process accordingly.

MORE COMPLETE ANSWER: This information could be stored in some other server not part of the normal audit log capture area.  Additionally, conduct regular backups to prevent intruders from manipulating logs; this will allow a means to compare changes, and identify potential incidents in the network for action by senior management or law enforcement.

| ASSESSMENT OBJECTIVE *Determine if:* | | |
|---|---|---|
| **SUB-CTRL** | **DESCRIPTION** | **RECOMMENDED APPROACH** |
| 3.3.8[a] | *Audit information is protected from unauthorized access.* | NCR |
| 3.3.8[b] | *Audit information is protected from unauthorized modification.* | NCR |
| 3.3.8[c] | *Audit information is protected from unauthorized deletion.* | NCR |
| 3.3.8[d] | *Audit logging tools are protected from unauthorized access.* | NCR |
| 3.3.8[e] | *Audit logging tools are protected from unauthorized modification.* | NCR |
| 3.3.8[f] | *Audit logging tools are protected from unauthorized deletion.* | NCR |

**ASSESSMENT METHODS AND CANDIDATE ARTIFACTS FOR REVIEW**

Examine: [*SELECT FROM:* Audit and accountability policy; access control policy and procedures; procedures addressing protection of audit information; system security plan; system design documentation; system configuration settings and associated documentation, system audit logs and records; audit logging tools; other relevant documents or records].

Test: [*SELECT FROM:* Mechanisms implementing audit information protection].

## 3.3.9 Limit management of audit functionality to a subset of privileged users.

MINIMUM ANSWER: See Control 3.3.8 for reducing the numbers of personnel with access to audit logs and functions. Maintaining a roster of personnel with appropriate user agreements can afford the ability to limit personnel as well as provide value in any future forensic activities required.

MORE COMPLETE ANSWER: There are several products such as CyberArk ® that could be used to manage and monitor privileged user access to audit information. This product will be a relatively expensive solution for small and some medium-sized C/U.

| ASSESSMENT OBJECTIVE *Determine if:* | | |
|---|---|---|
| **SUB-CTRL** | **DESCRIPTION** | **RECOMMENDED APPROACH** |
| 3.3.9[a] | *A subset of privileged users granted access to manage audit logging functionality is defined.* | NCR |
| 3.3.9[b] | *Management of audit logging functionality is limited to the defined subset of privileged users.* | NCR |

**POTENTIAL ASSESSMENT METHODS AND CANDIDATE ARTIFACTS FOR REVIEW**

Examine: [*SELECT FROM:* Audit and accountability policy; access control policy and procedures; procedures addressing protection of audit information; system security plan; system design documentation; system configuration settings and associated documentation; access authorizations; system-generated list of privileged users with access to management of audit logging functionality; access control list; system audit logs and records; other relevant documents or records].

Test: [*SELECT FROM:* Mechanisms managing access to audit logging functionality].

# CONFIGURATION MANAGEMENT (CM)
## The True Foundation of Cybersecurity

The real importance of Configuration Management is it is, in fact, the "opposite side of the same coin" called cybersecurity. CM is used to track and confirm changes to the system's baseline; this could be changed in hardware, firmware, and software that would alert IT professionals to unauthorized changes to the IT environment. CM is used to confirm and ensure programmatic controls prevent changes that have not been adequately tested or approved.

CM requires establishing baselines for tracking, controlling, and managing a C/U's internal IT infrastructure specific to NIST 800-171. Companies with an effective CM process need to consider information security implications for the development and operation of information systems. This will include the active management of changes to C/U hardware, software, and documentation.

Effective CM of information systems requires the integration of the management of secure configurations into the CM process. If good CM exists as a well-defined "change" process, protection of the IT environment is more assured. This should be considered as the second most important security control. It is suggested that both management and IT personnel have adequate knowledge and training to maintain this process since it is so integral to good programmatic and cyber security practice.

---

### Basic Security Requirements:

### 3.4.1 Establish and maintain baseline configurations and inventories of organizational information systems (including hardware, software, firmware, and documentation) throughout the respective system development life cycles.

MINIMUM ANSWER: This control can be best met by hardware, software, and firmware (should be combined with hardware) listings; these are the classic artifacts required for any system. Updating these documents as changes to the IT architecture is both a critical IT and logistics' functions. Ensure these staffs are well-coordinated about system changes. *This should be included in the System Security Plan (SSP).*

Also, NIST 800-171 requires document control of all reports, documents, manuals, etc. The currency of all related documents should be managed in a centralized repository.

Where documents may be sensitive, such as describing existing weaknesses or vulnerabilities of the IT infrastructure, these documents should have a greater level of control. The rationale for greater control of such documents is if these documents were "found" in the public, hackers or Advanced Persistent Threats (i.e., adversarial nation-states) could use to this information to conduct exploits. Vulnerabilities of C/U systems should be marked and controlled at least at the CUI/CDI level.

MORE COMPLETE ANSWER: Suggested better approaches to exercising good **version control** activities would be using a shared network drive, or a more advanced solution could use Microsoft ® SharePoint ®. An active version control tool should only allow authorized personnel to make changes to key documents and system changes and their associated **versioning**—major changes within the IT architecture, for example, from version 2.0 to 3.0. This should also maintain audit records of who and when a file is accessed and modified.

| ASSESSMENT OBJECTIVE *Determine if:* | | |
|---|---|---|
| **SUB-CTRL** | *DESCRIPTION* | **RECOMMENDED APPROACH** |
| **3.4.1[a]** | *A baseline configuration is established.* | NCR(SSP) - The SSP is the defined artifact to capture such information |
| **3.4.1[b]** | *The baseline configuration includes hardware, software, firmware, and documentation.* | NCR(SSP) |
| **3.4.1[c]** | *The baseline configuration is maintained (reviewed and updated) throughout the system development life cycle.* | P-Need to define and update as changes in configuration occur.  Who or what body updates and maintains the "baseline" specific to the SSP |
| **3.4.1[d]** | *A system inventory is established.* | NCR(SSP) |
| **3.4.1[e]** | *The system inventory includes hardware, software, firmware, and documentation.* | NCR(SSP) |
| **3.4.1[f]** | *The inventory is maintained (reviewed and updated) throughout the system development life cycle.* | P-See Sub-control 3.4.1[c] |

**ASSESSMENT METHODS AND CANDIDATE ARTIFACTS FOR REVIEW**

Examine: [*SELECT FROM:* Configuration management policy; procedures addressing the baseline configuration of the system; procedures addressing system inventory; system security plan; configuration management plan; system inventory records; inventory review and update records; enterprise architecture documentation; system design documentation; system architecture and configuration documentation; system configuration settings and associated documentation; change control records; system component installation records; system component removal records; other relevant documents or records].

Test: [*SELECT FROM:* Organizational processes for managing baseline configurations; mechanisms supporting configuration control of the baseline configuration; organizational processes for developing and documenting an inventory of system components; organizational processes for updating inventory of system components; mechanisms supporting or implementing the system inventory; mechanisms implementing updating of the system inventory].

## 3.4.2 Establish and enforce security configuration settings for information technology products employed in organizational information systems.

MINIMUM/MORE COMPLETE ANSWER: There should be an identification of any security configuration settings in C/U 's procedural documents. This would include technical policy settings, for example, number of failed logins, minimum password length, mandatory logoff settings, etc. These settings should be identified by a C/U 's Operating System, software application or program.

| ASSESSMENT OBJECTIVE *Determine if:* | | |
|---|---|---|
| **SUB-CTRL** | *DESCRIPTION* | **RECOMMENDED APPROACH** |
| **3.4.2[a]** | *Security configuration settings for information technology products employed in the system are established and included in the baseline configuration.* | P- *"Security configuration settings for information technology products employed in the system are established and included in the baseline configuration."* |
| **3.4.2[b]** | *Security configuration settings for information technology products employed in the system are enforced.* | P- *"Security configuration settings for information technology products employed in the system are enforced."* |
| **ASSESSMENT METHODS AND CANDIDATE ARTIFACTS FOR REVIEW** | | |

Examine: [*SELECT FROM:* Configuration management policy; baseline configuration; procedures addressing configuration settings for the system; configuration management plan; system security plan; system design documentation; system configuration settings and associated documentation; security configuration checklists; evidence supporting approved deviations from established configuration settings; change control records; system audit logs and records; other relevant documents or records].

Test: [*SELECT FROM:* Organizational processes for managing configuration settings; mechanisms that implement, monitor, and/or control system configuration settings; mechanisms that identify and/or document deviations from established configuration settings; processes for managing baseline configurations; mechanisms supporting configuration control of baseline configurations].

**Derived Security Requirements:**

## 3.4.3 Track, review, approve/disapprove, and audit changes to information systems.

MINIMUM ANSWER: This control addresses a defined C/U change *process*. This should be able to add or remove IT components within the network and provide needed currency regarding the state of the network. This should not be a purely IT staff function. If the firm can afford additional infrastructure personnel, it should assign a configuration manager; this person would administer the CM process.

MORE COMPLETE ANSWER: This could use Commercial Off the Shelf Technologies (COTS) that could be used to establish a more sophisticated CM database. This could also afford a more capable audit ability to prevent unauthorized changes.

| ASSESSMENT OBJECTIVE *Determine if:* | | |
|---|---|---|
| **SUB-CTRL** | *DESCRIPTION* | **RECOMMENDED APPROACH** |
| **3.4.3[a]** | *Changes to the system are tracked.* | NCR |
| **3.4.3[b]** | *Changes to the system are reviewed.* | NCR |
| **3.4.3[c]** | *Changes to the system are approved or disapproved.* | NCR |
| **3.4.3[d]** | *Changes to the system are logged.* | NCR |

**ASSESSMENT METHODS AND CANDIDATE ARTIFACTS FOR REVIEW**

Examine: [*SELECT FROM:* Configuration management policy; procedures addressing system configuration change control; configuration management plan; system architecture and configuration documentation; system security plan; change control records; system audit logs and records; change control audit and review reports; agenda/minutes from configuration change control oversight meetings; other relevant documents or records].

Test: [*SELECT FROM:* Organizational processes for configuration change control; mechanisms that implement configuration change control].

## 3.4.4 Analyze the security impact of changes prior to implementation.

MINIMUM ANSWER: Under NIST's risk management process, it requires that any changes to the baseline necessitate some level of technical analysis. This analysis is described as a **Security Impact Analysis (SIA),** and it is looking for any positive or negative changes that are considered **security relevant**.

This analysis should look at any change to the architecture, be it changes in hardware, software, firmware, or architecture. This should be described in the C/U CM process and could be as basic as a write-up from a member of the IT team, for example, that the change will or will not have a security impact, and it may or may not be security relevant.

If the change introduces a "negative" impact, such as eliminating backup capabilities or introducing currently unsupportable software (possibly due to funding constraints**), *it is the responsibility of the C/U to reinitiate the NIST 800-171 process in-full and advise the government of the rationale for the change.***

**See CM control 3.4.4 for a detailed Decision-tree.**

MORE COMPLETE ANSWER: A more-complete solution to this control would include, for example, the addition of a new software product that supports vulnerability scans using C/U anti-virus and malware applications or software products. Attach these reports as part of the record.

In the case of hardware updates, the C/U could demonstrate its SCRM process by attaching proof that the manufacturer is an authorized vendor approved by the government. Access to federal government Approved Products List (APL) may require the Contracting Officer Representative (COR) or Contracting Officer (CO) to approve access to specified databases. The positive review of these databases will demonstrate the proper level of due diligence for any current or future Authorization to Operate (ATO).

## 3.4.5 Define, document, approve, and enforce physical and logical access restrictions associated with changes to the information system.

MINIMUM/MORE COMPLETE ANSWER: "Access restrictions" are aligned with the earlier discussed AC controls. As part of a C/U CM policy, any changes to the IT baseline needs to be captured within a formal process approved by that process and documented.

Documentation is typically maintained in a CM database, and more specifically, it would require the update of any hardware or software lists. Proof of compliance would be the production of updated listings that are maintained by the CM database. This should include the updating of any network diagrams describing in a graphic form a description of the C/U network; these are all explicit requirements under NIST 800-171. These artifacts should also be included in the **SSP**.

| ASSESSMENT OBJECTIVE *Determine if:* | | |
|---|---|---|
| **SUB-CTRL** | *DESCRIPTION* | **RECOMMENDED APPROACH** |
| **3.4.5[a]** | *Physical access restrictions associated with changes to the system are defined.* | NCR |
| **3.4.5[b]** | *Physical access restrictions associated with changes to the system are documented.* | NCR |
| **3.4.5[c]** | *Physical access restrictions associated with changes to the system are approved.* | NCR |
| **3.4.5[d]** | *Physical access restrictions associated with changes to the system are enforced.* | NCR |
| **3.4.5[e]** | *Logical access restrictions associated with changes to the system are defined.* | NCR- ("Logical access" is described under Access Control is full). |
| **3.4.5[f]** | *Logical access restrictions associated with changes to the system are documented.* | NCR |
| **3.4.5[g]** | *Logical access restrictions associated with changes to the system are approved.* | NCR |
| **3.4.5[h]** | *Logical access restrictions associated with changes to the system are enforced.* | NCR |

## 3.4.6 Employ the principle of least functionality by configuring the information system to provide only essential capabilities.

MINIMUM ANSWER: Parts of the government have defined the use, for example, of File Transfer Protocol (FTP), Bluetooth, or peer-to-peer networking as insecure protocols. These protocols are unauthorized within many federal government environments, and companies seeking NIST 800-171 approval are best to follow this direction as well. Any written procedure should attempt to at least annually reassess whether a determination of the security of all functions, ports, protocols, or services are still correct.

MORE COMPLETE ANSWER: The use of automated network packet tools is recommended to conduct such reassessments. Ensure that IT personnel have the right experience and skill to provide a good analysis of this control requirement.

| ASSESSMENT OBJECTIVE *Determine if:* | | |
|---|---|---|
| **SUB-CTRL** | *DESCRIPTION* | **RECOMMENDED APPROACH** |
| **3.4.6[a]** | *Essential system capabilities are defined based on the principle of least functionality.* | NCR- (See earlier discussion regarding conducting an initial and annual Risk Assessment (RA)) |
| **3.4.6[b]** | *The system is configured to provide only the defined essential capabilities.* | NCR |

## 3.4.7 Restrict, disable, and prevent the use of nonessential programs, functions, ports, protocols, and services.

MINIMUM ANSWER: Nonessential programs, functions, ports, and protocols are prime attack avenues for would-be hackers. Any programs that are not used for the conduct of C/U operations should be removed.  Where that is not possible, these programs should be blacklisted to run in the C/U 's IT environment.  (See 3.4.8. below).

Regarding ports and protocols, this will require IT staff direct involvement in the decision-making process.  Certain ports are typically needed for any 21st Century C/U 's daily operation. For example, ports 80, 8080, and 443 are used to send HTTP (web traffic); these ports will typically be required to be active.

| Port Number | Application Supported |
|---|---|
| 20 | File Transport Protocol (FTP) Data |
| 23 | Telnet |
| 25 | Simple Mail Transfer Protocol (SMTP) |
| 80, 8080, 443 | Hypertext Transport Protocol (HTTP) → WWW |
| 110 | Post Office Protocol version 3 (POP3) |

**Common Ports and Their Associated Protocols**

For those ports and protocols that are not required, they should be closed by designated IT personnel.  This prevents hackers from exploiting open entries into the C/U infrastructure. Ensure a copy of all open and closed ports is readily available to government representatives for review as part of the NIST 800-171 requirements.

MORE COMPLETE ANSWER: The C/U could employ tools that check for unused and open ports. This could include a regular reassessment of whether ports need to remain active.  As mentioned earlier, products such as Wireshark ® could be used as a low-cost solution to conduct any reassessment of the C/U infrastructure.

| ASSESSMENT OBJECTIVE *Determine if:* | | |
|---|---|---|
| **SUB-CTRL** | *DESCRIPTION* | **RECOMMENDED APPROACH** |
| 3.4.7[a] | *Essential programs are defined.* | NCR (Always consult with Contract Office to determine any specified unauthorized programs, for example, "hacker tools," etc. |
| 3.4.7[b] | *The use of nonessential programs is defined.* | NCR |
| 3.4.7[c] | *The use of nonessential programs is restricted, disabled, or prevented as defined.* | NCR |
| 3.4.7[d] | *Essential functions are defined.* | NCR (artifact would include all "whitelisted" applications and functions) |
| 3.4.7[e] | *The use of nonessential functions is defined.* | NCR |

| | | |
|---|---|---|
| 3.4.7[f] | *The use of nonessential functions is restricted, disabled, or prevented as defined.* | NCR |
| 3.4.7[g] | *Essential ports are defined.* | NCR (Coordinate with Contract office at least annually regarding any updates to unauthorized ports). |
| 3.4.7[h] | *The use of nonessential ports is defined.* | NCR |
| 3.4.7[i] | *The use of nonessential ports is restricted, disabled, or prevented as defined.* | NCR |
| 3.4.7[j] | *Essential protocols are defined.* | NCR (Same as 3.4.7[g]) |
| 3.4.7[k] | *The use of nonessential protocols is defined.* | NCR |
| 3.4.7[l] | *The use of nonessential protocols is restricted, disabled, or prevented as defined.* | NCR |
| 3.4.7[m] | *Essential services are defined.* | NCR (Same as 3.4.7[g]) |
| 3.4.7[n] | *The use of nonessential services is defined.* | NCR |
| 3.4.7[o] | *The use of nonessential services is restricted, disabled, or prevented as defined.* | NCR |

**ASSESSMENT METHODS AND CANDIDATE ARTIFACTS FOR REVIEW**

Examine: [*SELECT FROM:* Configuration management policy; procedures addressing least functionality in the system; configuration management plan; system security plan; system design documentation; security configuration checklists; system configuration settings and associated documentation; specifications for preventing software program execution; documented reviews of programs, functions, ports, protocols, and/or services; change control records; system audit logs and records; other relevant documents or records].

Test: [*SELECT FROM:* Organizational processes for reviewing and disabling nonessential programs, functions, ports, protocols, or services; mechanisms implementing review and handling of nonessential programs, functions, ports, protocols, or services; organizational processes preventing program execution on the system; organizational processes for software program usage and restrictions; mechanisms supporting or implementing software program usage and restrictions; mechanisms preventing program execution on the system].

## 3.4.8 Apply deny-by-exception (blacklist) policy to prevent the use of unauthorized software or deny all, permit-by-exception (whitelisting) policy to allow the execution of authorized software.

MINIMUM/MORE COMPLETE ANSWER: The C/U should employ **blacklisting** or **whitelisting,** (See Control 3.14.2 for more information), to prohibit the execution of unauthorized software programs or applications within the information system. A copy of the current listing should be part of the formal Body of Evidence (BOE).

| ASSESSMENT OBJECTIVE *Determine if:* | | |
|---|---|---|
| **SUB-CTRL** | *DESCRIPTION* | **RECOMMENDED APPROACH** |
| **3.4.8[a]** | *A policy specifying whether whitelisting or blacklisting is to be implemented is specified.* | NCR |
| **3.4.8[b]** | *The software allowed to execute under whitelisting or denied use under blacklisting is specified.* | NCR |
| **3.4.8[c]** | *Whitelisting to allow the execution of authorized software or blacklisting to prevent the use of unauthorized software is implemented as specified.* | NCR |

**ASSESSMENT METHODS AND CANDIDATE ARTIFACTS FOR REVIEW**

Examine: [*SELECT FROM:* Configuration management policy; procedures addressing least functionality in the system; system security plan; configuration management plan; system design documentation; system configuration settings and associated documentation; list of software programs not authorized to execute on the system; list of software programs authorized to execute on the system; security configuration checklists; review and update records associated with list of authorized or unauthorized software programs; change control records; system audit logs and records; other relevant documents or records].

Test: [*SELECT FROM:* Organizational process for identifying, reviewing, and updating programs authorized or not authorized to execute on the system; process for implementing blacklisting or whitelisting; mechanisms supporting or implementing blacklisting or whitelisting].

## 3.4.9 Control and monitor user-installed software.

MINIMUM ANSWER: The policy should always be that only authorized administrators, such as designated SA's and senior help desk personnel, be allowed to add or delete software from user computers.

There should also be a defined process to request specialized software be added for unique users. These may include finance personnel, architects, statisticians, etc. that require specialized stand-alone software that may or may not connect to the Internet.

MORE COMPLETE ANSWER: This could include as part of the C/U 's normal audit processes the review of whether personnel is adding software and bypassing security measures (such as getting passwords from IT authorized individuals). This may also be addressed in the AUP and supported by appropriate HR activities that can be pursued against individuals of any such violations.

| ASSESSMENT OBJECTIVE *Determine if:* | | |
|---|---|---|
| **SUB-CTRL** | *DESCRIPTION* | **RECOMMENDED APPROACH** |
| **3.4.9[a]** | *A policy for controlling the installation of software by users is established.* | NCR |

| 3.4.9[b] | Installation of software by users is controlled based on the established policy. | NCR |
|----------|-----------------------------------------------------------------------------------|-----|
| 3.4.9[c] | Installation of software by users is monitored. | NCR |

**ASSESSMENT METHODS AND CANDIDATE ARTIFACTS FOR REVIEW**

Examine: [*SELECT FROM:* Configuration management policy; procedures addressing user installed software; configuration management plan; system security plan; system design documentation; system configuration settings and associated documentation; list of rules governing user-installed software; system monitoring records; system audit logs and records; continuous monitoring strategy; other relevant documents or records].

Test: [*SELECT FROM:* Organizational processes governing user-installed software on the system; mechanisms enforcing rules or methods for governing the installation of software by users; mechanisms monitoring policy compliance].

# IDENTIFICATION AND AUTHENTICATION (IA)
## Why two-factor authentication is so important?

The 2015 Office of Personnel Management (OPM) breach could have been prevented if this control family was properly implemented and enforced. The one "positive" effect that the OPM breach caused for federal agencies was the requirement from Congress that these requirements became mandatory. Congress's focus on the use of Two-Factor Authentication (2FA) and Multi-Factor Authentication (MFA) has provided constructive results for the federal government and impetus for more stringent cybersecurity measures beyond the government's IT boundaries.

While some C/U will be afforded, for example, Common Access Cards (CAC) or Personal Identity Verification (PIV) cards to accomplish 2FA between the C/U and the government, most won't be authorized such access. Implementation will require various levels of investment, and the use of 2FA devices, or also called "tokens." This too will require additional financial costs and technical integration challenges for the average C/U.

For many small C/U, this will also require some sizeable investments on the part of the C/U and a clear commitment to working with the government. Solutions could include, for example, RSA® tokens—these are small devices that constantly rotate a security variable (a key) that a user enters in addition to a password or Personal Identification Number (PIN). This solution affords one potential solution to C/U to meet the 2FA requirement.

---

*According to The House Committee on Oversight and Government Reform report on September 7th, 2016, OPM's leadership failed to "implement basic cyber hygiene, such as maintaining current authorities to operate and employing strong multi-factor authentication, despite years of warning from the Inspector General... tools were available that could have prevented the breaches..."* (SOURCE: https://oversight.house.gov/wp-content/uploads/2016/09/The-OPM-Data-Breach-How-the-Government-Jeopardized-Our-National-Security-for-More-than-a-Generation.pdf)

---

The best approaches will require good market surveys of the available resources and be mindful that two-factor does not need to be a card or token solution. Other options would include biometrics (fingerprints, facial recognition, etc.) or Short Message Service (SMS) 2FA solution as used by Amazon® to verify its customers. They use a Two-Step verification process that provides a "verification code sent to the customer's personal cell phone or home phone to verify their identity.

Be prepared to do serious "homework" on these controls, and research all potential solutions. Once this control is resolved, the C/U will be in a better position not just with the government but have serious answers that will ensure the protection of its sensitive data.

___

## Basic Security Requirements:

## 3.5.1 Identify information system users, processes acting on behalf of users, or devices.

MINIMUM/MORE COMPLETE ANSWER: This control should identify/reference current C/U procedures as outlined in the **AU** control above. It should address that audit is used to identify system users, the processes (applications) and the devices (computers) accessed.

| ASSESSMENT OBJECTIVE *Determine if:* | | |
|---|---|---|
| **SUB-CTRL** | *DESCRIPTION* | **RECOMMENDED APPROACH** |
| **3.5.1[a]** | *System users are identified.* | NCR |
| **3.5.1[b]** | *Processes acting on behalf of users are identified.* | NCR (through audit log collection) |
| **3.5.1[c]** | *Devices accessing the system are identified.* | NCR |
| **ASSESSMENT METHODS AND CANDIDATE ARTIFACTS FOR REVIEW** Examine: [*SELECT FROM:* Identification and authentication policy; procedures addressing user identification and authentication; system security plan, system design documentation; system configuration settings and associated documentation; system audit logs and records; list of system accounts; other relevant documents or records]. Test: [*SELECT FROM:* Organizational processes for uniquely identifying and authenticating users; mechanisms supporting or implementing identification and authentication capability]. | | |

## 3.5.2 Authenticate (or verify) the identities of those users, processes, or devices, as a prerequisite to allowing access to organizational information systems.

MINIMUM ANSWER: While basic logon and password information could be used, Control 3.5.3 below, requires Multifactor or Two-factor Authentication (2FA). The government requires 2FA, and NIST 800-171 requires it as well.

**Remember, if the C/U is not immediately prepared to execute a 2FA solution, *a POAM is required*.

MORE COMPLETE ANSWER: The better answer is the employment of some form of 2FA. It could be a **hard token** solution such as a CAC or PIV card. The other option would include such virtual solutions that would use email or SMS messaging like Google ® or Amazon ® to provide 2FA; this **soft token** solution is typically easier and less expensive to deploy.   It can be more easily deployed to meet NIST 800-171 requirement.

| ASSESSMENT OBJECTIVE *Determine if:* | | |
|---|---|---|
| **SUB-CTRL** | *DESCRIPTION* | **RECOMMENDED APPROACH** |
| **3.5.2[a]** | *The identity of each user is authenticated or verified as a prerequisite to system access.* | NCR |
| **3.5.2[b]** | *The identity of each process acting on behalf of a user is authenticated or verified as a prerequisite to system access.* | NCR |
| **3.5.2[c]** | *The identity of each device accessing or connecting to the system is authenticated or verified as a prerequisite to system access.* | P/T/PO/W- This will require policy and potential technical control updates where, for example, servers are authenticating to other servers securely. This may require a POAM or waiver in certain time-restricted circumstances. |

**ASSESSMENT METHODS AND CANDIDATE ARTIFACTS FOR REVIEW**

Examine: [*SELECT FROM:* Identification and authentication policy; system security plan; procedures addressing authenticator management; procedures addressing user identification and authentication; system design documentation; list of system authenticator types; system configuration settings and associated documentation; change control records associated with managing system authenticators; system audit logs and records; other relevant documents or records].

Test: [*SELECT FROM:* Mechanisms supporting or implementing authenticator management capability].

## Derived Security Requirements:

### 3.5.3 Use multifactor authentication for local and network access to privileged accounts and for network access to non-privileged accounts.

MINIMUM ANSWER:  See Control 3.5.2 above.  Ensure the requirement for MFA or 2FA are part of the C/U 's cybersecurity policy/procedure.

MORE COMPLETE ANSWER: (See Control 3.5.2 for suggested approaches).

| ASSESSMENT OBJECTIVE *Determine if:* | | |
|---|---|---|
| **SUB-CTRL** | *DESCRIPTION* | **RECOMMENDED APPROACH** |
| **3.5.3[a]** | *Privileged accounts are identified.* | NCR |
| **3.5.3[b]** | *Multifactor authentication is implemented for local access to privileged accounts.* | NCR (At least two-factor authentication; Windows 10® allows for biometric facial recognition—a potential small architecture solution for many) |

| 3.5.3[c] | *Multifactor authentication is implemented for network access to privileged accounts.* | NCR |
|---|---|---|
| 3.5.3[d] | *Multifactor authentication is implemented for network access to non-privileged accounts.* | NCR |

**ASSESSMENT METHODS AND CANDIDATE ARTIFACTS FOR REVIEW**

Examine: [*SELECT FROM:* Identification and authentication policy; procedures addressing user identification and authentication; system security plan; system design documentation; system configuration settings and associated documentation; system audit logs and records; list of system accounts; other relevant documents or records].

Test: [*SELECT FROM:* Mechanisms supporting or implementing multifactor authentication capability].

## 3.5.4 Employ replay-resistant authentication mechanisms for network access to privileged and nonprivileged accounts.

MINIMUM ANSWER: This control requires replay-resistant technologies to prevent replay attacks. **Replay attacks** are also known as a **playback attack**. This is an attack where the hacker captures legitimate traffic from an authorized user, and presumably a positively identified network user, and uses it to gain unauthorized access to a network. This is also considered a form of a **Man-in-the-Middle** type attack.

The easiest solution to resolving this control is to have C/U IT personnel disable **Secure Socket Layer (SSL)**—which the government no longer authorizes. C/U should use the **Transport Layer Security (TLS) 2.0** or higher; it as a required government standard.

If the C/U needs to continue the use of SSL to maintain connectivity with, for example, external or third-party data providers, a POAM is required. Efforts should be made to discuss with these data providers when they will no longer be using SSL. This discussion should begin as soon as possible to advise the government through a POAM that demonstrates the C/U is conducting its proper due diligence to protect its CUI/CDI.

MORE COMPLETE ANSWER: A potentially expensive solution could include the addition of a **SIEM** solution. There are many major IT network providers that have added artificial intelligence capabilities to detect this type of attack better; identify any solution carefully.

## 3.5.5 Prevent reuse of identifiers for a defined period.

MINIMUM ANSWER: This IA control directs that "individual, group, role, or device identifiers" from being reused. This should be included as part of any written procedure and defined in system policies to prevent identifiers from being reused. This could include email address names (individual), administrator accounts (group), or device identifiers such as "finan_db" designating a high-value target such as a "financial database" (device).

The reason for this control is to prevent intruders who have gained information about such identifiers having less of a capability to use this information for an exploit of the C/U. This will help better thwart hacker's intelligence collection and analysis of a C/U 's internal network. This control is designed to prevent intruders' abilities to gain access to C/U systems and their resident CUI/CDI repositories.

MORE COMPLETE ANSWER: Reuse of individual identifiers should be discouraged, for example, in the case of a returning employee. This is a basic suggestion: 'John.Smith@cui-C/U .com' could be varied examples, 'John.H.Smith2@cui-C/U .com.

| ASSESSMENT OBJECTIVE *Determine if:* | | |
|---|---|---|
| **SUB-CTRL** | *DESCRIPTION* | **RECOMMENDED APPROACH** |
| **3.5.5[a]** | *A period within which identifiers cannot be reused is defined.* | NCR |
| **3.5.5[b]** | *Reuse of identifiers is prevented within the defined period.* | NCR |

**ASSESSMENT METHODS AND CANDIDATE ARTIFACTS FOR REVIEW**
Examine: [*SELECT FROM:* Identification and authentication policy; procedures addressing identifier management; procedures addressing account management; system security plan; system design documentation; system configuration settings and associated documentation; list of system accounts; list of identifiers generated from physical access control devices; other relevant documents or records].

Test: [*SELECT FROM:* Mechanisms supporting or implementing identifier management].

## 3.5.6 Disable identifiers after a defined period of inactivity.

MINIMUM/MORE COMPLETE ANSWER: This requires that after a defined time-out setting, the system terminates its connection. The recommendation is 30 minutes maximum, but as mentioned earlier, the time-out should always be based on the data sensitivity.

| ASSESSMENT OBJECTIVE *Determine if:* | | |
|---|---|---|
| **SUB-CTRL** | *DESCRIPTION* | **RECOMMENDED APPROACH** |
| **3.5.6[a]** | *A period of inactivity after which an identifier is disabled is defined.* | NCR |
| **3.5.6[b]** | *Identifiers are disabled after the defined period of inactivity.* | NCR |

**POTENTIAL ASSESSMENT METHODS AND CANDIDATE ARTIFACTS FOR REVIEW**
Examine: [*SELECT FROM:* Identification and authentication policy; procedures addressing identifier management; procedures addressing account management; system security plan; system design documentation; system configuration settings and associated documentation; list of system accounts; list of identifiers generated from physical access control devices; other relevant documents or records].

Test: [*SELECT FROM:* Mechanisms supporting or implementing identifier management].

## 3.5.7 Enforce a minimum password complexity and change of characters when new passwords are created.

MINIMUM ANSWER: If using passwords for authentication purposes, the expectation is that a POAM has been developed until such time a 2FA or MFA solution is in place. The standard complexity is supposed to be at least 15 characters that include at least 2 or more alpha, numeric, and special characters to reduce the likelihood of compromise.

MORE COMPLETE ANSWER: Increased length and variability can be enforced by automated policy settings of the network. Another suggestion is to use passphrases. These can be harder to "crack" by normal hacking tools and are typically easier for users to memorize.

| ASSESSMENT OBJECTIVE *Determine if:* | | |
|---|---|---|
| **SUB-CTRL** | *DESCRIPTION* | **RECOMMENDED APPROACH** |
| **3.5.7[a]** | *Password complexity requirements are defined.* | NCR |
| **3.5.7[b]** | *Password change of character requirements are defined.* | NCR |
| **3.5.7[c]** | *Minimum password complexity requirements as defined are enforced when new passwords are created.* | NCR (Consult with Contract Office specific to DOD's 15-character alpha-numeric requirement) |
| **3.5.7[d]** | *Minimum password changes of character requirements as defined are enforced when new passwords are created.* | NCR |

**ASSESSMENT METHODS AND CANDIDATE ARTIFACTS FOR REVIEW**

Examine: [*SELECT FROM:* Identification and authentication policy; password policy; procedures addressing authenticator management; system security plan; system configuration settings and associated documentation; system design documentation; password configurations and associated documentation; other relevant documents or records].

Test: [*SELECT FROM:* Mechanisms supporting or implementing password-based authenticator management capability].

### *The best solutions are still either 2FA or MFA*

The factors:

- **1-FACTOR:** Something you know (e.g., password/PIN)
- **2-FACTOR:** Something you have (e.g., cryptographic identification device, token)

- MULTI-FACTOR: Something you are (e.g., biometric: fingerprint, iris, etc.)

---

## 3.5.8 Prohibit password reuse for a specified number of generations.

MINIMUM ANSWER: This is usually set by policy and the designated SA's that limit the number of times a password can be reused; *passwords within most parts of the government are required to be changed every 90 days.* This function should be automated by authorized IT personnel.  Suggested reuse of a prior password should be at least 10 or greater

MORE COMPLETE ANSWER: Technical settings can be established for *no* reuse.  This ensures that hackers who may have exploited one of the user's other C/U or even (and more especially) personal accounts, can less likely to be effective against C/U computer networks and assets.

| ASSESSMENT OBJECTIVE *Determine if:* | | |
|---|---|---|
| **SUB-CTRL** | *DESCRIPTION* | **RECOMMENDED APPROACH** |
| **3.5.8[a]** | *The number of generations during which a password cannot be reused is specified.* | NCR |
| **3.5.8[b]** | *Reuse of passwords is prohibited during the specified number of generations.* | NCR |
| **ASSESSMENT METHODS AND CANDIDATE ARTIFACTS FOR REVIEW**<br>Examine: [*SELECT FROM:* Identification and authentication policy; password policy; procedures addressing authenticator management; system security plan; system design documentation; system configuration settings and associated documentation; password configurations and associated documentation; other relevant documents or records].<br>Test: [*SELECT FROM:* Mechanisms supporting or implementing password-based authenticator management capability]. | | |

## 3.5.9 Allow temporary password use for system logons with an immediate change to a permanent password.

MINIMUM/MORE COMPLETE ANSWER: This setting is typically built into normal network operating systems.  This requirement for users should be appropriately included in the recommended procedure guide.

## 3.5.10 Store and transmit only encrypted representation of passwords.

MINIMUM ANSWER:  This is both a DIT and DAR issue, See Control 3.1.3 for a conceptual diagram.  IT personnel should be regularly verifying that password data stores are always encrypted.

This control requires that all passwords are encrypted and approved by NIST's sanctioned process under FIPS 140-2. See Control 3.13.11 for the NIST website to confirm whether a cryptographic solution is approved.

MORE COMPLETE ANSWER: Suggested greater protections could require encrypted passwords are not collocated on the same main application or database server that stores major portions of the C/U 's data repository. A separate server (physical or virtual) could prevent hacker exploits from accessing C/U data stores.

| ASSESSMENT OBJECTIVE *Determine if:* | | |
|---|---|---|
| SUB-CTRL | *DESCRIPTION* | RECOMMENDED APPROACH |
| 3.5.10[a] | *Passwords are cryptographically protected in storage.* | NCR |
| 3.5.10[b] | *Passwords are cryptographically protected in transit.* | NCR |
| ASSESSMENT METHODS AND CANDIDATE ARTIFACTS FOR REVIEW<br>Examine: [*SELECT FROM:* Identification and authentication policy; password policy; procedures addressing authenticator management; system security plan; system configuration settings and associated documentation; system design documentation; password configurations and associated documentation; other relevant documents or records].<br>Test: [*SELECT FROM:* Mechanisms supporting or implementing password-based authenticator management capability]. | | |

## 3.5.11. Obscure feedback of authentication information.

MINIMUM/MORE COMPLETE ANSWER: This is like **pattern hiding** as described in Control 3.1.10. The system should prevent unauthorized individuals from compromising system-level authentication by inadvertently observing in-person ("shoulder surfing") or virtually (by viewing password entries by privileged users) remotely. It relies upon obscuring the "feedback of authentication information", for example, displaying asterisks (*) or hash symbols (#) when a user types their password. This setting should be enforced automatically and prevent general users from changing this setting.

# INCIDENT RESPONSE (IR)
## What do you do when you're attacked?

Incident Response (IR) primarily requires a plan, an identification of who or what agency is notified when a breach has occurred and testing of the plan over time. This control requires the development of an Incident Response Plan (IRP). There are many templates available online, and if there is an existing relationship with a federal agency, companies should be able to obtain agency-specific templates.

---

# EVENT → INCIDENT
### (less defined/initial occurrence) → (defined/confirmed/high impact)

### Incident Response Spectrum

---

The first effort should be identifying with government representatives what constitutes a reportable event that formally becomes an incident. This could include a confirmed breach that has occurred to the IT infrastructure. Incidents could include anything from a Denial of Service (DOS) attack—an overloading of outwardly facing web or mail servers--, or exfiltration of data—where CUI/CDI and C/U data has been copied or moved to outside of the C/U 's firewall/perimeter. Incidents could also include the destruction of data that the C/U 's IT staff, for example, identifies through ongoing audit activities.

Secondarily, who do you notify? Do you alert your assigned Contract Officer Representative (COR), the Contract Office, DOD's US Cybercommand at Fort Meade, MD, or possibly the Department of Homeland Security's (DHS) Computer Emergency Response Team (CERT) (https://www.us-cert.gov/forms/report)? C/U representatives will have to ask their assigned COR where to file standard government "incident" reports. They should be able to provide templates and forms specific to the agency.

Finally, this security control will require testing at least *annually*, but more often is recommended. Until comfortable with the IR "reporting chain," *practice, practice, practice*.

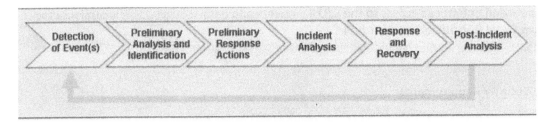

**DOD Cyber Incident Life Cycle.** This diagram from the DOD is a representative example of a typical "incident response life cycle." It is intended to assist in a C/U's approach to IR activities, and will better assist in coordination with government cybersecurity incident response organizations. Recognizing this as either an "event" (not necessarily a negative occurrence) versus an "incident" is an internal determination by the C/U's leadership in coordination with its security and IT professional staffs. An incident specifically requires alerting the government as soon as the intrusion is *recognized*.

Verify with the respective agency its reporting standards. Typically, **events** may not need to be reported based on the expansive impacts and workloads to government cybersecurity response organizations. In the case of **incidents**, the standard is 72-hours; however, the recommendation is *as soon as possible* due to the potential impacts beyond the C/U's own IT infrastructure. It can pose a serious direct threat to federal agency IT environments. Always verify this with the assigned Contract Office representative.

The chart below categorizes current DOD and DHS common precedence designations. It provides both a standard categorization for identified events and typically, precedence is used to identify the level of action and response depending on the precedence "severity."

| Precedence | Category | Description |
|---|---|---|
| 0 | 0 | Training and Exercises |
| 1 | 1 | Root Level Intrusion (Incident) |
| 2 | 2 | User Level Intrusion (Incident) |
| 3 | 4 | Denial of Service (Incident) |
| 4 | 7 | Malicious Logic (Incident) |
| 5 | 3 | Unsuccessful Activity Attempt (Event) |
| 6 | 5 | Non-Compliance Activity (Event) |
| 7 | 6 | Reconnaissance (Event) |
| 8 | 8 | Investigating (Event) |
| 9 | 9 | Explained Anomaly (Event) |

**DOD Precedence Categorization.** Nine (9) is the lowest event where little is known, and IT personnel are attempting to determine whether this activity should be elevated to alert C/U leadership or to "close it out." One (1) is a deep attack. It identifies that the incident has gained "root" access. Root access can be construed as that the intruder has complete access to the most restrictive security levels of a system. This type of access usually is construed to complete and unfettered access to the C/U 's network and data. (SOURCE: Cyber Incident Handling Program, CJCSM 6510.01B, 18 December 2014, http://www.jcs.mil/Portals/36/Documents/Library/Manuals/m651001.pdf?ver=2016-02-05-175710-897)

**Basic Security Requirements:**

## 3.6.1 Establish an operational incident-handling capability for organizational information systems that includes adequate preparation, detection, analysis, containment, recovery, and user response activities.

MINIMUM ANSWER: This control addresses a "capability" that needs to be established to respond to events and incidents within the firm's IT security boundary.

This should include the **People, Process, and Technology (PPT) Model** as a recommended guide for answering many of the controls within NIST 800-171. While solutions will not necessarily require a technological answer, consideration of the people (e.g., who? what skill sets? etc.) and process (e.g., notifications to senior management, action workflows, etc.) will meet many of the response requirements.

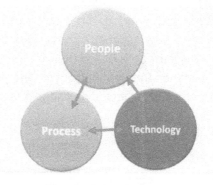

**PPT Model**

Use the Cyber Incident **Life Cycle** above to guide the C/U 's operational incident-handling artifact/procedure. This should be an annex to the **SSP**. (See System Security Plan (SSP) Template and Workbook: A Supplement to "DOD NIST 800-171 Compliance Guidebook" on Amazon®). The **PPT Model** can be used to guide and formulate the IRP annex. A suggested approach using the PPT Model is described below, and includes the kinds of questions that should be answered to demonstrate best how best to formulate a good IRP:

- Preparation
    - People: Who will perform the action or activity? Training needed? Skill sets?
    - Process: Training policies for cybersecurity and IT professionals to support the IRP

- Technology: What technology already exists to support IR? What technologies are needed?

- Detection
  - People: Are IT staff able to use audit tools properly to detect intrusions?
  - Process: What are 'best practice' approaches to detect intrusions? Monitor firewall logs? Monitor user activity?
  - Technology: Is the technology's data library current? Are automatic updates enabled?

- Analysis
  - People: Are IT staff capable to do the analysis required? Can they determine false positive activity?
  - Process: What is the process leadership wants to get effective and actionable data from IT staff? What are the demands for immediate and final reporting timelines?
  - Technology: Are the right tools on-site? Can open source/web solutions useful? Can DOD or DHS provide helpful data feeds to remain current of threats?

- Containment
  - People: Can IT staff stop the ongoing attack? Do they require additional coding scripting skills to build/update firewall policies?
  - Process: Is the containment process effective? Is allowing the attack to continue to identify the threat entity/location a good idea (to support law enforcement)?
  - Technology: Can software tools quarantine and stop a malware attack? Is shutting down all external connections a good immediate solution (at the firewall)?

- Recovery Actions
  - People: Can the IT staff recover backup data files and media?
  - Process: What is the order of recovery? Bring up internal databases and communications first and external servers (email and web site) be reestablished later? What are the recovery time standards for the C/U to regain C/U operations? What is acceptable? What is not acceptable?
  - Technology: Are there adequate numbers of back up devices for critical systems? Can third-party service providers assist in recovering lost or damaged data?

- User Response Activities
  - People: Can employees safely return to an operational state?

- o Process: Does the C/U need to control access to services to select individuals first (e.g., finance, logistics, etc.)
- o Technology: Can technology resolve immediate problems from the recovery vice the employee such as, for example, reselecting printers and other data connections?

MORE COMPLETE ANSWER: In those situations when control is specifically discussing a policy solution, the employment of automated tools, alerts, etc., should always be considered. Even the use of basic tracking tools such as Microsoft ® Excel ® and Access ® will at least demonstrate a level of positive control over the IT environment.

| ASSESSMENT OBJECTIVE *Determine if:* | | |
|---|---|---|
| **SUB-CTRL** | **DESCRIPTION** | **RECOMMENDED APPROACH** |
| **3.6.1[a]** | *An operational incident-handling capability is established.* | NCR |
| **3.6.1[b]** | *The operational incident-handling capability includes preparation.* | NCR |
| **3.6.1[c]** | *The operational incident-handling capability includes detection.* | NCR |
| **3.6.1[d]** | *The operational incident-handling capability includes analysis.* | NCR/PO/W- (It may be unreasonable for a small C/U to have any analytic capability other than collection of logs and referral to the agency for action; a Waiver may be absolutely needed) |
| **3.6.1[e]** | *The operational incident-handling capability includes containment.* | NCR |
| **3.6.1[f]** | *The operational incident-handling capability includes recovery.* | NCR |
| **3.6.1[g]** | *The operational incident-handling capability includes user response activities.* | NCR |

**ASSESSMENT METHODS AND CANDIDATE ARTIFACTS FOR REVIEW**

Examine: [*SELECT FROM:* Incident response policy; contingency planning policy; procedures addressing incident handling; procedures addressing incident response assistance; incident response plan; contingency plan; system security plan; procedures addressing incident response training; incident response training curriculum; incident response training materials; incident response training records; other relevant documents or records].

Test: [*SELECT FROM:* Incident-handling capability for the organization; organizational processes for incident response assistance; mechanisms supporting or implementing incident response assistance].

## 3.6.2 Track, document, and report incidents to appropriate officials and/or authorities both internal and external to the organization.

MINIMUM ANSWER: This control discusses the reporting requirements based on the severity of the incident as described above in DOD's Precedence Categorization diagram. Ensure some form of the repository is maintained that an auditor could review at any time. Another reminder is that such information should be secured and encrypted at least at the CUI/CDI level.

MORE COMPLETE ANSWER: A more complete response may include a dedicated computer server repository that could be physically disconnected from the system when not needed. This could prevent unauthorized access if an intruder is attempting to conduct intelligence collection or **reconnaissance** of the system; this would deny intruders critical network information and add confusion for their penetration activities.

| ASSESSMENT OBJECTIVE *Determine if:* | | |
|---|---|---|
| **SUB-CTRL** | *DESCRIPTION* | **RECOMMENDED APPROACH** |
| **3.6.2[a]** | *Incidents are tracked.* | NCR |
| **3.6.2[b]** | *Incidents are documented.* | NCR |
| **3.6.2[c]** | *Authorities to whom incidents are to be reported are identified.* | NCR |
| **3.6.2[d]** | *Organizational officials to whom incidents are to be reported are identified.* | NCR |
| **3.6.2[e]** | *Identified authorities are notified of incidents.* | NCR |
| **3.6.2[f]** | *Identified organizational officials are notified of incidents.* | NCR |

**ASSESSMENT METHODS AND CANDIDATE ARTIFACTS FOR REVIEW**

Examine: [SELECT FROM: Incident response policy; procedures addressing incident monitoring; incident response records and documentation; procedures addressing incident reporting; incident reporting records and documentation; incident response plan; system security plan; other relevant documents or records].

Test: [SELECT FROM: Incident monitoring capability for the organization; mechanisms supporting or implementing tracking and documenting of system security incidents; organizational processes for incident reporting; mechanisms supporting or implementing incident reporting].

## Derived Security Requirements:

## 3.6.3 Test the organizational incident response capability.

MINIMUM ANSWER: Test the IR Plan at least annually. This should include both internal and external notional penetration exercises. These may include compromised login information and passwords provided to designated IT personnel. Ensure the results of the test are documented, reviewed, and signed by senior management. An IR test event should be maintained for any future audit.

MORE COMPLETE ANSWER: This is not a requirement of this control and poses many risks to the IT environment. Do not recommend this solution; this would only be required based on the sensitivity of data, and Penetration Testing (PENTEST) is directed by the government. It is only offered for more of an appreciation of the complexity that a PENTEST entails.

A more expensive solution is hiring an outside Penetration Testing (PENTEST) C/U. Ensure that Rules of Engagement (ROE) are well established. Rules that should be affirmed by both the C/U and the PENTESTER, for example, is that no inadvertent change or destruction of data is authorized. The PENTEST C/U may also require a liability release for any unintentional damage caused by the PENTEST. Always coordinate with legal professionals experienced in such matters to avoid any damage or confusion created by unclear expectations of a PENTEST.

# MAINTENANCE (MA)
## How do you take care of IT?

The MA security control is relatively easy to address with regards to the requirements of NIST 800-171. This control requires processes and procedures that provide oversight of third-party vendors that offer IT maintenance and support. While this may appear vaguely paranoid, the C/U is required to exercise control of all maintenance personnel that potentially will have access to the C/U 's and government's resident CUI/CDI and data. This will also typically require C/U escorts whose background have been properly checked and authorized to oversee outside workers.

Lack of maintenance or a failure to perform maintenance can result in the unauthorized disclosure of CUI/CDI. The full implementation of this requirement is contingent on the finalization of the proposed CUI/CDI federal regulation and marking guidance in the **CUI Registry**. (The marking requirements have been completed, and it is best to refer to the Registry, https://www.archives.gov/cui/registry/category-list, for specified industry codes.) These markings should be applied to C/U CUI/CDI data as well as IT hardware such as servers, desktops, laptops, etc.

**Basic Security Requirements:**

## 3.7.1 Perform maintenance on organizational information systems.

MINIMUM ANSWER: This should describe the C/U 's maintenance procedures for its IT infrastructure. This could include either internal maintenance teams or third-party companies. This will include hardware component repairs and replacements, printer repairs, etc. Any maintenance agreements should be provided as artifacts to support an authorization package.

MORE COMPLETE ANSWER: Maintenance could include the identification of computer hardware spares on-site or at C/U warehouse locations. Operational spares should be managed by the C/U 's logistics' personnel; they should be captured within the property book database and its associated hard copy reporting to senior management.

## 3.7.2 Provide effective controls on the tools, techniques, mechanisms, and personnel used to conduct information system maintenance.

MINIMUM ANSWER: This control relates to tools used for diagnostics and repairs of the C/U 's IT system/network. These tools include, for example, hardware/software diagnostic test equipment and hardware/software **packet sniffers**. Access to the hardware tools should be secured in lockable containers, and only accessed by authorized IT personnel.

In the case of software tools, they should be restricted to personnel with privileged user rights and specifically audited when any use is required or needed.

MORE COMPLETE ANSWER: Suggested additional control may include two-person integrity requirements. This would require that when any of these types of tools are utilized, there should be at least two authorized individuals involved in any system maintenance or diagnostic activities.

| ASSESSMENT OBJECTIVE *Determine if:* | | |
|---|---|---|
| **SUB-CTRL** | *DESCRIPTION* | **RECOMMENDED APPROACH** |
| **3.7.2[a]** | *Tools used to conduct system maintenance are controlled.* | NCR |
| **3.7.2[b]** | *Techniques used to conduct system maintenance are controlled.* | NCR |
| **3.7.2[c]** | *Mechanisms used to conduct system maintenance are controlled.* | NCR |
| **3.7.2[d]** | *Personnel used to conduct system maintenance are controlled.* | NCR |

**ASSESSMENT METHODS AND CANDIDATE ARTIFACTS FOR REVIEW**

Examine: [*SELECT FROM:* System maintenance policy; procedures addressing system maintenance tools and media; maintenance records; system maintenance tools and associated documentation; maintenance tool inspection records; system security plan; other relevant documents or records].

Test: [*SELECT FROM:* Organizational processes for approving, controlling, and monitoring maintenance tools; mechanisms supporting or implementing approval, control, and monitoring of maintenance tools; organizational processes for inspecting maintenance tools; mechanisms supporting or implementing inspection of maintenance tools; organizational process for inspecting media for malicious code; mechanisms supporting or implementing inspection of media used for maintenance].

## Derived Security Requirements:

### 3.7.3 Ensure equipment removed for off-site maintenance is sanitized of any CUI.

MINIMUM ANSWER: C/U data should be backed-up locally and secured for a future reinstall on another storage device or on the returned/repaired IT component. Also, the data should specifically be "wiped" by an industry-standard application for data deletion. There are many software tools that conduct multiple "passes" of data wipes to ensure sanitization of the media.

MORE COMPLETE ANSWER: Any reports produced by the data "wiping" program could be captured in an equipment data log to provide proof of the action. Maintaining a hard copy of soft copy spreadsheet or database log would be helpful. Future inspections by the government may check this procedure to confirm the continuous application and repeatability of this procedure.

### 3.7.4 Check media containing diagnostic and test programs for malicious code before the media are used in the information system.

MINIMUM ANSWER: The normal solution for this is to conduct a scan using C/U anti-virus software applications.

MORE COMPLETE ANSWER: A more thorough solution would include the use of an anti-malware application. Anti-malware programs are more comprehensive and proactively monitor **endpoints**, i.e., computers, laptops, servers, etc. (Anti-virus is not always designed to identify and clean malware, adware, worms, etc., from infected storage devices).

### 3.7.5 Require multifactor authentication to establish nonlocal maintenance sessions via external network connections and terminate such connections when nonlocal maintenance is complete.

MINIMUM ANSWER: Nonlocal maintenance are those diagnostic or repair activities conducted over network communications to include the Internet or dedicated least circuits.

This requires that any external third-party maintenance activities use some form of Multi-Factor Authentication (MFA) to directly access C/U IT hardware and software components. If IT personnel, working with outside maintainers can use an MFA solution then the C/U most likely has a robust IT support capability. If not, then this control is a good candidate for an early POAM; ensure good milestones are established for monthly review, for example, "on-going research," "market survey of potential candidate solutions," "identification of funding sources," etc.

MORE COMPLETE ANSWER: A more complete answer requires a technical solution. As discussed earlier, the use of CAC, PIV cards, or tokens, such as the RSA ® rotating encryption keying devices are ideal solutions. This solution most likely will require additional analysis and funding approaches to select the most appropriate answer.

RSA Token (R)

| ASSESSMENT OBJECTIVE *Determine if:* | | |
|---|---|---|
| **SUB-CTRL** | **DESCRIPTION** | **RECOMMENDED APPROACH** |
| **3.7.5[a]** | *Multifactor authentication is used to establish nonlocal maintenance sessions via external network connections.* | NCR |
| **3.7.5[b]** | *Nonlocal maintenance sessions established via external network connections are* | NCR |

| | |
|---|---|
| *terminated when nonlocal maintenance is complete.* | |

**ASSESSMENT METHODS AND CANDIDATE ARTIFACTS FOR REVIEW**

Examine: [*SELECT FROM:* System maintenance policy; procedures addressing nonlocal system maintenance; system security plan; system design documentation; system configuration settings and associated documentation; maintenance records; diagnostic records; other relevant documents or records].

Test: [*SELECT FROM:* Organizational processes for managing nonlocal maintenance; mechanisms implementing, supporting, and managing nonlocal maintenance; mechanisms for strong authentication of nonlocal maintenance diagnostic sessions; mechanisms for terminating nonlocal maintenance sessions and network connections].

## 3.7.6 Supervise the maintenance activities of maintenance personnel without required access authorization.

MINIMUM ANSWER:  The procedure requirement should reflect that non-C/U maintenance personnel should always be escorted.  An access log should be maintained, and it should include, for example, the individual or individuals, the represented C/U, the equipment repaired/diagnosed, the arrival and departure times, and the assigned escort. Maintain this hard-copy of soft-copy logs for future auditing purposes.

MORE COMPLETE ANSWER: Procedural enhancements could include confirmed background checks of third-party maintainers and picture identification compared with the on-site individual.  These additional enhancements should be based upon the sensitivity of the C/U's data.  Any unattended CUI/CDI data should always be secured by CUI/CDI procedures—in a lockable container.

# MEDIA PROTECTION (MP)
## Create, protect, and destroy

The MP control was written to handle the challenges of managing and protecting the computer media storing CUI/CDI. This would include the governments' concerns about removable hard drives and especially the ability for a threat employ the use of a Universal Serial Bus (USB) "thumb drive."

While most computer users are aware of the convenience of the thumb drive to help store, transfer, and maintain data, it is also a well-known threat vector where criminals and foreign threats can introduce serious malware and viruses into unsuspecting users' computers; the DOD forbids their use except under very specific and controlled instances.

MP is also about assurances by the C/U that proper destruction and sanitization of old storage devices has occurred. There are many instances where federal agencies have not implemented an effective sanitization process, and inadvertent disclosure of national security data has been released to the public. Cases include salvage companies discovering hard drives and disposed computers containing CUI/CDI and, in several cases, national security classified information, has occurred.

Be especially mindful that the sanitization process requires high-grade industry or government-approved applications that completely and effectively destroys all data on the target drive. Other processes may include physical shredding of the drive or destruction methods that further prevent the reconstruction of any virtual data by unauthorized personnel.

---

## Basic Security Requirements:

### 3.8.1 Protect (i.e., physically control and securely store) information system media containing CUI, both paper and digital.

MINIMUM ANSWER: To implement this control the C/U should establish procedures regarding both CUI/CDI physical and virtual (disk drives) media. This should include only authorized personnel having access to individual and C/U sensitive data with requisite background checks and training. A C/U can use the foundations of other control families to further **mitigate** or reduce risks/threats.

A C/U can use other controls such as *more* training, longer audit log retention, *more* guards, or *more* complex passwords to **mitigate** any control. This would more clearly demonstrate to the government that the firm has a positive implementation of these security controls.

### RISK MANAGEMENT'S FOUNDATION:

MITIGATE OR REDUCE,
NOT ELIMINATION
OF THE RISK OR THREAT

The use of other mitigating controls within NIST 800-171 are specifically about **risk reduction.** Any effort to use other families of controls to meet a specific control improves the overall IT infrastructure's security posture and is highly recommended.

MORE COMPLETE ANSWER: The MP control can be further demonstrated by safeguarding physical files in secure or fire-resistant vaults. This could also include requirements for only IT personnel issuing property hand receipts for computer equipment or devices; a good accountability system is important.

| ASSESSMENT OBJECTIVE *Determine if:* | | |
|---|---|---|
| **SUB-CTRL** | *DESCRIPTION* | **RECOMMENDED APPROACH** |
| **3.8.1[a]** | *Paper media containing CUI is physically controlled.* | NCR |
| **3.8.1[b]** | *Digital media containing CUI is physically controlled.* | NCR |
| **3.8.1[c]** | *Paper media containing CUI is securely stored.* | NCR (Typically demonstrated by securing within a lockable container, desk, etc., and the individual/s authorized access are the only one's identified to enter, remove, or destroy CUI data from its holding area.) |
| **3.8.1[d]** | *Digital media containing CUI is securely stored.* | NCR |

**ASSESSMENT METHODS AND CANDIDATE ARTIFACTS FOR REVIEW**

Examine: [SELECT FROM: System media protection policy; procedures addressing media storage; procedures addressing media access restrictions; access control policy and procedures; physical and environmental protection policy and procedures; system security plan; media storage facilities; access control records; other relevant documents or records].

Test: [SELECT FROM: Organizational processes for restricting information media; mechanisms supporting or implementing media access restrictions].

### 3.8.2 Limit access to CUI on information system media to authorized users.

MINIMUM ANSWER: Identify in policy documents who, by name, title or function, has access to specified CUI/CDI. Any artifacts should include the policy document and an associated by-name roster of personnel assigned access by-system, e.g., accounting system, ordering system, patent repository, medical records, etc.

MORE COMPLETE ANSWER: A more complete response could include logging of authorized personnel and providing a print-out of accesses over a one-month period.

### 3.8.3 Sanitize or destroy information system media containing CUI before disposal or release for reuse.

MINIMUM ANSWER: A good policy description is a must regarding data destruction of sensitive information within the government. Either use a commercial-grade "wiping" program, or physically destroy the drive.

If the C/U is either planning to internally reuse or sell to outside repurposing companies, ensure that the wiping is commercial grade or approved by the government. There are companies providing disk shredding or destruction services. Provide any service agreements that should specify the type and level of data destruction to government assessors.

NIST Special Publication 800-161

Supply Chain Risk Management
Practices for Federal Information
Systems and Organizations

MORE COMPLETE ANSWER: For any assessment, the media sanitization C/U should provide **destruction certificates**. Chose several selected destruction certificates to include in the BOE submission. Typically, logistics and supply ordering sections of the C/U should manage as part of the Supply Chain Risk Management (SCRM) process.

| ASSESSMENT OBJECTIVE *Determine if:* | | |
|---|---|---|
| **SUB-CTRL** | ***DESCRIPTION*** | **RECOMMENDED APPROACH** |
| **3.8.3[a]** | *System media containing CUI is sanitized or destroyed before disposal.* | NCR |
| **3.8.3[b]** | *System media containing CUI is sanitized before it is released for reuse.* | NCR |

**ASSESSMENT METHODS AND CANDIDATE ARTIFACTS FOR REVIEW**

Examine: [*SELECT FROM:* System media protection policy; procedures addressing media sanitization and disposal; applicable standards and policies addressing media sanitization; system security plan; media sanitization records; system audit logs and records; system design documentation; system configuration settings and associated documentation; other relevant documents or records].

Test: [*SELECT FROM:* Organizational processes for media sanitization; mechanisms supporting or implementing media sanitization].

---

## A QUICK SIDE DISCUSSION ON SUPPLY CHAIN RISK MANAGEMENT

**SCRM** is a relatively new concern within the federal government. It is part of securing IT products within the C/U.

Questions that should be considered include:

- Is this product produced by the US or by an Ally?
- Could counterfeit IT items be purchased from less-than reputable entities?
- Is this IT product from an approved hardware/software product listing?

Users innately trust software developers to provide secure updates for their software applications and products that would add new functionalities or fix security vulnerabilities. They would not expect updates to be infected with malicious scripts, codes or programming. Most users have no mechanisms (or no concerns) about defending against seemingly legitimate software that is properly signed. Unfortunately, software unwittingly accessed by users and tainted by either nation-state actors or general cyber-criminals on the Internet pose an alarming risk to the global IT supply chain.

The use of varied supply chain attacks by cyber attackers to access C/U software development infrastructures have been major vectors of concerns for the government as well as private sector. These attacks typically include targeting publicly connected software build, test, update servers, and other portions of a software C/U's software development environment. Nation-state agents can then inject malware into software updates and releases have far-ranging impacts to the IT supply chain; the challenge continues to grow.[3]

Users become infected through official software distribution channels that are trusted. Attackers can add their malware to the development infrastructure of software vendors before they are compiled[4], hence, the malware is signed with the digital identity of a legitimate software vendor. This exploit bypasses typical "whitelisting" security measures making it difficult to identify the intrusion. This has contributed to a high degree of success by malicious cyber threat actors. Some example recent intrusions include:

- In July 2017, Chinese cyber espionage operatives changed the software packages of a legitimate software vendor, NetSarang Computer (https://www.netsarang.com/). These changes allowed access to a broad range of industries and institutions that included retail locations, financial services, transportation, telecommunications, energy, media, and academic.

- In August 2017, hackers inserted a backdoor into updates of the computer "cleanup" program, **CCleaner** while it was in its software development phases.

- In June 2017, suspected Russian actors **deployed the** PETYA ransomware to a wide-range of European targets by compromising a targeted Ukrainian software vendor

Another recent example of a supply chain compromise occurred in 2017. During this incident, Dell **lost** control of a customer support website and its associated Internet web address. Control of the website was wrested from a Dell support contractor that had failed to renew its authorized domain license and fees. The site was designed specifically to assist customers in the restoration of their computer and its data when infected. There were subsequent signs that the domain may have been infecting customers; two weeks after the contractor lost control of the address, the server that hosted the domain began appearing in numerous malware alerts.

The site was purchased by **TeamInternet.com,** a German company that specializes in Uniform Resource Locator (URL) hijacking and typosquatting[5] type exploits. (This company could also sell or lease the domain to anyone at that point to include back to Dell). They took advantage of users believing they were going to a legitimate site and then being redirected to this redesigned

---

[3] Other less-protected portions of the supply chain include, for example, Field Programmable Gate Arrays (FPGA) and Application-Specific Integrated Circuit (ASIC) chips found on most major US weapons and satellite systems.

[4] Before they are converted as an executable (.exe) that are injected at the programming level where quality control mechanisms are often less-than adequate in secure development processes

[5] **Typosquatting** is a form of Uniform Resource Locator (URL) hijacking, and also can be described as a form of cybersquatting and possibly brandjacking (e.g., Pepsie.com). It relies on mistakes by the individual especially due to "typos." It causes redirects using subtle and common variations in spellings to both malicious and marketing (adware) sites.

malware site.

Supply chain compromises have been seen for years, but they have been mostly isolated and covert[6] in nature. They may follow with subsequent intrusions into targets of interest much later and provide a means for general hacking and damage to the C/U targets. The use of such a compromise provides highly likely means to support nation-state cyberespionage activities including those identified from Chinese IT equipment product builders. These include such companies such Chinese-based companies to include ZTE, Lenovo, and Huawei.

This trend continues to grow as there are more points in the supply chain that the attackers can penetrate using advance techniques. The techniques involved have become publicly discussed enough, and their proven usefulness encourages others to use these vectors of attack specific to damage and reconnaissance of governments, C/U and agencies globally. Advanced actors will likely continue to leverage this activity to conduct cyber espionage, cybercrime, and disruption. The dangers to the supply chain are of growing concern as the threat and risk landscapes continue to increase for the foreseeable future.

For further information see NIST 800-161, *Supply Chain Risk Management Practices for Federal Information Systems and Organizations.*
( http://nvlpubs.nist.gov/nistpubs/SpecialPublications/NIST.SP.800-161.pdf ).

---

**Derived Security Requirements:**

## 3.8.4 Mark media with necessary CUI markings and distribution limitations.
MINIMUM ANSWER: This includes the marking of both physical documents as well as soft-copy versions. The best way to answer this is by referencing the following National Archives and Record Administration (NARA) document as part of the C/U 's procedural guide that addresses this control:

- *Marking Controlled Unclassified Information*, Version 1.1 – December 6, 2016.
  (https://www.archives.gov/files/cui/20161206-cui-marking-handbook-v1-1.pdf )

  *EXAMPLE PROCEDURE: All C/U personnel will mark CUI/CDI, physical and virtual data, in accordance with the National Archives and Record Administration (NARA), Marking Controlled Unclassified Information, Version 1.1 – December 6, 2016. If there are questions about marking requirements, employees will refer these questions to their immediate supervisor or the C/U CUI/CDI officer."*

---

[6] Disclosing such information by a C/U may have both legal and reputation impacts; current US law under the 2015 Computer Information Security Act (CISA) does allow for "safe harbor" protections in the US.

MORE COMPLETE ANSWER: This could include a screen capture that shows a government representative that onscreen access to CUI/CDI data is properly marked. A firm could also assign a CUI/CDI marking specialist; this person should be an individual with prior security experience and familiar with marking requirements. For example, this individual could additionally provide quarterly "brown bag" sessions where the "CUI/CDI Security Officer" provides training during lunchtime sessions. Be creative when considering more thorough means to reinforce cybersecurity control requirements.

| ASSESSMENT OBJECTIVE *Determine if:* | | |
|---|---|---|
| **SUB-CTRL** | *DESCRIPTION* | **RECOMMENDED APPROACH** |
| **3.8.4[a]** | *Media containing CUI is marked with applicable CUI markings.* | NCR |
| **3.8.4[b]** | *Media containing CUI is marked with distribution limitations.* | NCR |
| **ASSESSMENT METHODS AND CANDIDATE ARTIFACTS FOR REVIEW** | | |
| Examine: [*SELECT FROM:* System media protection policy; procedures addressing media marking; physical and environmental protection policy and procedures; system security plan; list of system media marking security attributes; designated controlled areas; other relevant documents or records]. | | |
| Test: [*SELECT FROM:* Organizational processes for marking information media; mechanisms supporting or implementing media marking]. | | |

## 3.8.5 Control access to media containing CUI and maintain accountability for media during transport outside of controlled areas.

MINIMUM ANSWER:  This control is about "transport outside of controlled areas." This too is a matter of only authorized individuals (couriers) be authorized by position, training, and security checks that should be considered when the C/U needs to transport CUI/CDI external to its typical C/U location.

Individuals should be provided either courier cards or orders that are signed by an authorized C/U representative typically responsible for oversight of security matters.  This could be, for example, the C/U security officer, Information System Security Manager (ISSM), or their designated representative. These individuals should be readily known to other employees and managers who have demanded to move CUI/CDI to outside locations. This would demonstrate there is available and on-call personnel based on the C/U mission and priorities.  This also should be a limited cadre of personnel that management relies on for such external courier services.

MORE COMPLETE ANSWER: The C/U could hire an outside contract service that transports both physical and computer media containing CUI/CDI based on the C/U 's mission.

| ASSESSMENT OBJECTIVE *Determine if:* | | |
|---|---|---|
| **SUB-CTRL** | *DESCRIPTION* | **RECOMMENDED APPROACH** |
| **3.8.5[a]** | *Access to media containing CUI is controlled.* | NCR |
| **3.8.5[b]** | *Accountability for media containing CUI is maintained during transport outside of controlled areas.* | NCR |

**ASSESSMENT METHODS AND CANDIDATE ARTIFACTS FOR REVIEW**

Examine: [*SELECT FROM:* System media protection policy; procedures addressing media storage; physical and environmental protection policy and procedures; access control policy and procedures; system security plan; system media; designated controlled areas; other relevant documents or records].

Test: [*SELECT FROM:* Organizational processes for storing media; mechanisms supporting or implementing media storage and media protection].

## 3.8.6 Implement cryptographic mechanisms to protect the confidentiality of CUI stored on digital media during transport unless otherwise protected by alternative physical safeguards.

MINIMUM ANSWER: This is a Data at Rest (DAR) issue. See Control 3.1.3 for depiction. The recommendation is that all CUI/CDI needs to be encrypted. A common application that has been used is BitLocker ®. It provides password protection to "lock down" any transportable media. It is not the only solution, and there are many solutions that can be used to secure DAR.

The 256-bit key length is the common standard for commercial and government encryption applications for hard drives, removable drives, and even USB devices. The government requires DAR must always be encrypted; it is best to resource and research acceptable tools that the government supports and recognizes.

MORE COMPLETE ANSWER: The reinforcing of this control may include using enhanced physical security measures. This could include hardened and lockable carry cases. Only authorized employees should transport designated CUI/CDI. This should also be captured in the submitted BOE.

## 3.8.7 Control the use of removable media on information system components.

MINIMUM ANSWER: Identify in C/U policy the types and kinds of removable media that can be attached to fixed desktop and laptop computers. These could include external hard drives, optical drives, or USB thumb drives.

Strongly recommend that thumb drives are not used; if needed, then designate IT security personnel who can authorize their restricted use. This should also include anti-virus/malware scans before their use.

MORE COMPLETE ANSWER: Removeable media drives can be "blocked" by changes in system **registry** settings; C/U IT personnel should be able to prevent such designated devices from accessing the computer and accessing the C/U network.

### 3.8.8 Prohibit the use of portable storage devices when such devices have no identifiable owner.

MINIMUM ANSWER: This should be established in the C/U procedure. If such devices are found, they should be surrendered to security, and scanned immediately for any viruses, malware, etc.

MORE COMPLETE ANSWER: As described in Control 3.8.7, IT personnel can block unauthorized devices from attaching to the computer/network by updating registry settings.

### 3.8.9 Protect the confidentiality of backup CUI at storage locations.

MINIMUM ANSWER: *This is a Data at Rest (DAR) issue.* See Control 3.1.3 for a depiction. See Control 3.8.6 for suggested requirements for the protection of CUI/CDI under a DAR solution.

MORE COMPLETE ANSWER: See Control 3.8.6 for additional means to protect CUI/CDI.

# PERSONNEL SECURITY (PS)
## Background Checks

This is a relatively simple control. It most likely is already implemented within the C/U and only requires procedural documents are provided in the submission. This should include both civil and criminal background checks using a reputable company that can process the individual background checks through the Federal Bureau of Investigation (FBI). Background Checking companies can also do other forms of personnel checks to include individual social media presence or financial solvency matters that may avoid any future embarrassment for the C/U.

While these checks are not well defined for C/U's under NIST 800-171, it should meet minimum government standards for a **Public Trust** review. Discuss with the Contract Officer what the requirements they suggest be met to provide the level of background check required to meet the NIST 800-171 requirement. Also, it is always best to work with HR and legal experts when formulating a personnel security policy to include the types and kinds of investigations are in accordance with applicable state and federal law in this area.

---

## Basic Security Requirements:

### 3.9.1 Screen individuals prior to authorizing access to information systems containing CUI.
MINIMUM ANSWER: This control requires some form of background check be conducted for employees. There are number of firms that can provide criminal and civil background checks based upon individual's personal information and their fingerprints.

The C/U should capture its HR process regarding background checks in the C/U cybersecurity procedure document. It's also important to address when a reinvestigation is required. The suggestion is at least every 3 years or upon recognition by managers of potential legal occurrences that may include financial problems, domestic violence, etc. This control should be highly integrated with the C/U HR and legal policies.

MORE COMPLETE ANSWER: Some background companies can, for an additional fee, conduct active monitoring of individuals when major personal or financial changes occur in a person's life. Update C/U procedural guides with all details of the C/U's established process.

## 3.9.2 Ensure that CUI and information systems containing CUI are protected during and after personnel actions such as terminations and transfers.

MINIMUM ANSWER: This control is about procedures regarding whether termination is amicable or not. Always have clear terms about non-removal of C/U data and CUI/CDI after departure from the C/U to include databases, customer listings, and proprietary data/IP. This should include legal implications for violation of the policy.

MORE COMPLETE ANSWER: The technical solution could include monitoring by IT staff of all account activity during the out-processing period. This could also include immediate account lock-outs on the departure date. Also recommend that there are changes to all vault combinations, building accesses, etc., that the individual had specific access to during their tenure.

| ASSESSMENT OBJECTIVE *Determine if:* | | |
|---|---|---|
| **SUB-CTRL** | *DESCRIPTION* | **RECOMMENDED APPROACH** |
| **3.9.2[a]** | *A policy and/or process for terminating system access and any credentials coincident with personnel actions is established.* | NCR |
| **3.9.2[b]** | *System access and credentials are terminated consistent with personnel actions such as termination or transfer.* | NCR |
| **3.9.2[c]** | *The system is protected during and after personnel transfer actions.* | P- An update should include changes or updates in accesses when an employee transfers to another location or office. |

**ASSESSMENT METHODS AND CANDIDATE ARTIFACTS FOR REVIEW**
Examine: [*SELECT FROM:* Personnel security policy; procedures addressing personnel transfer and termination; records of personnel transfer and termination actions; list of system accounts; records of terminated or revoked authenticators and credentials; records of exit interviews; other relevant documents or records].
Test: [*SELECT FROM:* Organizational processes for personnel transfer and termination; mechanisms supporting or implementing personnel transfer and termination notifications; mechanisms for disabling system access and revoking authenticators].

**Derived Security Requirements:** None.

# PHYSICAL PROTECTION (PP)
## Guards and moats....

Physical security is part of a C/U's overall protection of its people and facilities. A little-known fact is that the guiding principle for any *true* cybersecurity professional is to protect the life and safety of the people supported. This control is also about the protection of damage to C/U assets, facilities, or equipment; this includes any loss or destruction of the material computer equipment secured by the PP security control. This controls addresses the physical security that also includes such elements as guards, alarm systems, cameras, etc., that help the C/U protect its sensitive C/U data and, of course, its NIST 800-171 CUI.

There are no limits on how to harden a C/U's "castle walls," but for any owner, the cost is always a major consideration. Protecting vital CUI/CDI while seemingly expansive under this control allows for reasonable flexibility. Again, the C/U should reasonably define its success under the NIST 800-171 controls. "Success" can be defined from the C/U's point of view regarding complexity or cost but must be prepared to defend any proposed solution to government assessors.

---

**Basic Security Requirements:**

**3.10.1 Limit physical access to organizational information systems, equipment, and the respective operating environments to authorized individuals.**
MINIMUM ANSWER: Of importance for this control, is limiting access to C/U data servers, backup devices, and specifically, the "computer farm." If the C/U is maintaining devices on its premises, then policy should address who has authorized access to such sensitive areas.

If the C/U is using an off-site **Cloud Service Provider (CSP)**, capture in part or full sections of any CSP service agreements specific to physical security measures. Both types of computer architectures should address for example areas of interest such as access logs, after-hours access, camera monitoring, unauthorized access reporting criteria, types and kinds of network defense devices such as Intrusion Detection and Prevention Systems (IDS/IPS), etc., as part of the C/U procedure.

MORE COMPLETE ANSWER: This could include active alerting to both management and security personnel that includes phone calls, email alerts, or SMS text messages to designated C/U security personnel. Security measures and **alert thresholds** should be driven by the sensitivity of the data stored. Management should make **risk-based** determinations of the cost and returns on effectiveness to drive the C/U policy for this control as well as other solutions.

| ASSESSMENT OBJECTIVE *Determine if:* | | |
|---|---|---|
| **SUB-CTRL** | *DESCRIPTION* | **RECOMMENDED APPROACH** |
| **3.10.1[a]** | *Authorized individuals allowed physical access are identified.* | NCR |
| **3.10.1[b]** | *Physical access to organizational systems is limited to authorized individuals.* | NCR |
| **3.10.1[c]** | *Physical access to equipment is limited to authorized individuals.* | NCR |
| **3.10.1[d]** | *Physical access to operating environments is limited to authorized individuals.* | NCR |

**ASSESSMENT METHODS AND CANDIDATE ARTIFACTS FOR REVIEW**

Examine: [*SELECT FROM:* Physical and environmental protection policy; procedures addressing physical access authorizations; system security plan; authorized personnel access list; authorization credentials; physical access list reviews; physical access termination records and associated documentation; other relevant documents or records].

Test: [*SELECT FROM:* Organizational processes for physical access authorizations; mechanisms supporting or implementing physical access authorizations].

## 3.10.2 Protect and monitor the physical facility and support infrastructure for those information systems.

MINIMUM/MORE COMPLETE ANSWER: This control can be addressed in many ways by physical security measures. This should include locked doors, cipher locks, safes, security cameras, guard forces, etc. This control should be answered by the current physical protections that prevent direct entry into the C/U and physical access to its IT devices and networks.

| ASSESSMENT OBJECTIVE *Determine if:* | | |
|---|---|---|
| **SUB-CTRL** | *DESCRIPTION* | **RECOMMENDED APPROACH** |
| **3.10.2[a]** | *The physical facility where organizational systems reside is protected.* | NCR |
| **3.10.2[b]** | *The support infrastructure for organizational systems is protected.* | NCR- (This would include all physical barriers to entries into computer spaces, server rooms, etc., for unauthorized personnel) |
| **3.10.2[c]** | *The physical facility where organizational systems reside is monitored.* | NCR - (typically, cameras or guards) |
| **3.10.2[d]** | *The support infrastructure for organizational systems is monitored.* | NCR |

## Derived Security Requirements:

### 3.10.3 Escort visitors and monitor visitor activity.

MINIMUM ANSWER: Much as described under the MA control above, like security measures as described in Control 3.7.6 should be employed.

MORE COMPLETE ANSWER:  Also, refer to Control 3.7.6 on greater security measures that can be used to demonstrate more complete compliance with this control.

| SUB-CTRL | DESCRIPTION | RECOMMENDED APPROACH |
|---|---|---|
| **ASSESSMENT OBJECTIVE** *Determine if:* | | |
| **3.10.3[a]** | *Visitors are escorted.* | NCR |
| **3.10.3[b]** | *Visitor activity is monitored.* | NCR – (Escorts, guards, and cameras inclusive) |

ASSESSMENT METHODS AND CANDIDATE ARTIFACTS FOR REVIEW

Examine: [SELECT FROM: Physical and environmental protection policy; procedures addressing physical access control; system security plan; physical access control logs or records; inventory records of physical access control devices; system entry and exit points; records of key and lock combination changes; storage locations for physical access control devices; physical access control devices; list of security safeguards controlling access to designated publicly accessible areas within facility; other relevant documents or records].

Test: [SELECT FROM: Organizational processes for physical access control; mechanisms supporting or implementing physical access control; physical access control devices].

### 3.10.4 Maintain audit logs of physical access.

MINIMUM/MORE COMPLETE ANSWER: Refer to Control 3.7.6 for suggested audit log items. This should address personnel during operating and after hour entry into the C/U and its IT facilities.  This should include logs specific to outside third-party vendors and subcontractors; any such procedures should also apply to those individuals who are not direct employees.

### 3.10.5 Control and manage physical access devices.

MINIMUM ANSWER:  This control requires that physical access devices such as security badges, combinations, and physical keys are managed through both procedure and logs (physical or automated). The C/U needs to demonstrate to the government its positive security measures to protect its CUI/CDI data. While this control may appear easier than the technical policy control settings used by the C/U for its IT systems, it is no less important.

MORE COMPLETE ANSWER: If not already in place, identify and separate the physical security functions (e.g., facility security officer, etc.) from the technical security functions managed by C/U IT personnel with the requisite skills and experiences. Companies should avoid duty-creep on its cybersecurity personnel and define roles and responsibilities between its classic security functions (e.g., physical, personnel security, etc.) and the roles and responsibilities of its cyber workforce that may reduce their effectiveness of both security areas.

| ASSESSMENT OBJECTIVE *Determine if:* | | |
|---|---|---|
| **SUB-CTRL** | *DESCRIPTION* | **RECOMMENDED APPROACH** |
| **3.10.5[a]** | *Physical access devices are identified.* | NCR |
| **3.10.5[b]** | *Physical access devices are controlled.* | NCR |
| **3.10.5[c]** | *Physical access devices are managed.* | NCR |

**ASSESSMENT METHODS AND CANDIDATE ARTIFACTS FOR REVIEW**

Examine: [SELECT FROM: Physical and environmental protection policy; procedures addressing physical access control; system security plan; physical access control logs or records; inventory records of physical access control devices; system entry and exit points; records of key and lock combination changes; storage locations for physical access control devices; physical access control devices; list of security safeguards controlling access to designated publicly accessible areas within facility; other relevant documents or records].

Test: [SELECT FROM: Organizational processes for physical access control; mechanisms supporting or implementing physical access control; physical access control devices].

---

*Cybersecurity workforce duty-creep is a real-world occurrence; Companies are unwittingly shifting overall "security" functions from classic security personnel to cybersecurity professionals creating security gaps for a C/U*

---

3.10.6 Enforce safeguarding measures for CUI at alternate work sites (e.g., telework sites).

MINIMUM ANSWER: (See Control 3.1.3 for the explanation of DAR and DIT). This control can be easily addressed by DAR application solutions. Laptops should always be password protected;

this should be part of any central cybersecurity policy document and enforced by technical solutions deployed by C/U IT personnel. Additionally, The DIT protections are afforded by C/U VPN and 2FA/MFA solutions.

MORE COMPLETE ANSWER: The C/U should establish minimum requirements for telework protection. This could include, for example, work should be conducted in a physically securable area, the VPN should always be used, C/U assets should not use unsecured networks such as at coffee shops, fast-food restaurants, etc. This could also include an explicit telework agreement for employees before being authorized telework permission, and it should be closely coordinated with HR and legal experts.

| ASSESSMENT OBJECTIVE *Determine if:* | | |
|---|---|---|
| **SUB-CTRL** | *DESCRIPTION* | **RECOMMENDED APPROACH** |
| **3.10.6[a]** | *Safeguarding measures for CUI are defined for alternate work sites.* | NCR |
| **3.10.6[b]** | *Safeguarding measures for CUI are enforced for alternate work sites.* | NCR |

**ASSESSMENT METHODS AND CANDIDATE ARTIFACTS FOR REVIEW**

Examine: [*SELECT FROM:* Physical and environmental protection policy; procedures addressing alternate work sites for personnel; system security plan; list of safeguards required for alternate work sites; assessments of safeguards at alternate work sites; other relevant documents or records].

Test: [*SELECT FROM:* Organizational processes for security at alternate work sites; mechanisms supporting alternate work sites; safeguards employed at alternate work sites; means of communications between personnel at alternate work sites and security personnel].

# RISK ASSESSMENT (RA)
## Dealing with Changes to the Infrastructure

The RA control relies on a continual process to determine whether changes in hardware, software or architecture create either a major positive or negative **security-relevant** effect. This is typically done by using a **Change Request** (CR). If an upgrade to, for example, the Window 10 ® Secure Host Baseline Operating System software, and it improves the security posture of the network, a Risk Assessment (RA) is needed and associated **risk analysis** should be performed by authorized technical personnel. This could take the form of a technical report that management accepts from its IT staff for approval or disapproval of the change. Management, working with its IT staff, should determine thresholds when a formal RA activity needs to occur.

The RA process affords a great amount of flexibility during the life of the system and should be used when other-than, for example, a new application or **security patches** are applied. Security patches updates are typically integrated into Operating Systems and applications. IT personnel should also regularly manually check for normal functional patches and security patch updates from the software companies' websites.

"Negative" security-relevant effects on the C/U IT infrastructure include, for example, a major re-architecture event or a move to a Cloud Service Provider. While these events may not seem "negative," NIST standards require a full reassessment. In other words, plan accordingly if the C/U is going to embark on a major overhaul of its IT system. There will be a need under these circumstances to consider the impacts to the C/U 's current Authority to Operate (ATO). These types of event typically necessitate that the NIST 800-171 process is redone; prior work in terms of policies and procedures can be reused to receive an updated ATO.

The decision-tree below is designed to help a C/U determine when to consider an RA:

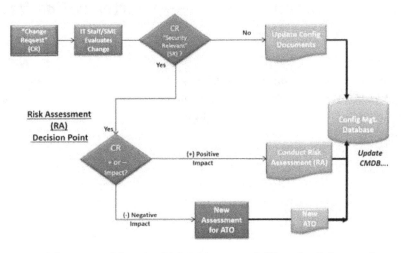

**Decision-tree Addressing Risk Assessment & "Security Relevance"**

**Basic Security Requirements:**

**3.11.1 Periodically assess the risk to organizational operations (including mission, functions, image, or reputation), organizational assets, and individuals, resulting from the operation of organizational information systems and the associated processing, storage, or transmission of CUI.**

MINIMUM ANSWER: RA's are required when there is a "major" change due to either a hardware change (e.g., replacing an old firewall with a new Cisco ® firewall), software version upgrades (e.g., moving from Adobe ® 8.0 to 9.0), or changes to architecture (e.g., adding a new backup drive). The consideration is always about *how* this change to the baseline configuration is either a positive (normal) or negative (preferably, highly unlikely)?

It is important to describe the C/U RA process in terms of change needed and overall risk to the IT system. This should include who conducts the technical portion of the RA and who, in senior management, for example, the Chief Operating Officer (COO) or Chief Information Officer (CIO) that determines final approval.

> *This is as new to Federal Contracting as it is to the C/U; understand there will be "growing pains," as the government continues to better define its procedures*

While not thoroughly discussed as part of this book, *the integration of the NIST 800-171 with federal government contracting is in its infancy*. It is best to coordinate and advise the government Contract Officers of any changes. It is always "best practice" to maintain a history of RA development and approval for future auditing.

MORE COMPLETE ANSWER: Implementing a more defined RA process could include standardized formats for RA artifacts. This could include a technical report written by knowledgeable IT personnel about a change, or a simplified form that allows for a checklist-like approach. It could also employ an outside third-party C/U that would formalize a review of the changes and their analysis of the overall impact to system security.

| SUB-CTRL | DESCRIPTION | RECOMMENDED APPROACH |
|---|---|---|
| 3.11.1[a] | *The frequency to assess risk to organizational operations, organizational assets, and individuals is defined.* | NCR – (See discussion above regarding RA's conducted annually) |
| 3.11.1[b] | *Risk to organizational operations, organizational assets, and individuals resulting from the operation of an organizational system that processes, stores, or transmits CUI is assessed with the defined frequency.* | NCR |

**ASSESSMENT METHODS AND CANDIDATE ARTIFACTS FOR REVIEW**

Examine: [*SELECT FROM:* Risk assessment policy; security planning policy and procedures; procedures addressing organizational risk assessments; system security plan; risk assessment; risk assessment results; risk assessment reviews; risk assessment updates; other relevant documents or records].

Test: [*SELECT FROM:* Organizational processes for risk assessment; mechanisms supporting or for conducting, documenting, reviewing, disseminating, and updating the risk assessment].

## Derived Security Requirements:

**3.11.2 Scan for vulnerabilities in the information system and applications periodically and when new vulnerabilities affecting the system are identified.**

MINIMUM ANSWER: This control requires that the C/U (system owner) regularly scans for vulnerabilities in the information system and hosted applications based upon a defined frequency or randomly based upon an established policy or procedure. This is also supposed to be applied when new vulnerabilities affecting the system or applications are identified.

> **Reminder**
>
> **Supply Chain Risk Management (SCRM)**
>
> The Russian-based software developer, Kaspersky Lab's ® Anti-virus solutions are currently prohibited.

The simplest way to address this control is using **anti-virus** and **anti-malware** enterprise-levels of software versions. Major players in these areas include Symantec ®, McAfee ®, and Malwarebytes ®. Procedural documents should describe the products used to address "new vulnerabilities" using these solutions. See also SYSTEM AND INFORMATION INTEGRITY (SI) as a reinforcing control for this RA control.

MORE COMPLETE ANSWER: A suggested more complete implementation could be the leveraging of C/U ISP services also is identified for providing a secondary layer of defense as a form of "trusted" connection. This could include any available SLA's that define the service provider's ability to mitigate such additional threats by employing **whitelisting** and **blacklisting** services; these services are designed to allow or restrict access depending on an **Access Control List** (ACL). See Control 3.14.2 for a more detailed description.

| ASSESSMENT OBJECTIVE *Determine if:* | | |
|---|---|---|
| **SUB-CTRL** | *DESCRIPTION* | **RECOMMENDED APPROACH** |
| **3.11.2[a]** | *The frequency to scan for vulnerabilities in organizational systems and applications is defined.* | NCR |
| **3.11.2[b]** | *Vulnerability scans are performed on organizational systems with the defined frequency.* | NCR |
| **3.11.2[c]** | *Vulnerability scans are performed on applications with the defined frequency.* | NCR – (typically monthly, but more often for major virus releases or "zero-day" threats) |
| **3.11.2[d]** | *Vulnerability scans are performed on organizational systems when new vulnerabilities are identified.* | NCR |
| **3.11.2[e]** | *Vulnerability scans are performed on applications when new vulnerabilities are identified.* | NCR |

**ASSESSMENT METHODS AND CANDIDATE ARTIFACTS FOR REVIEW**

Examine: [*SELECT FROM:* Risk assessment policy; procedures addressing vulnerability scanning; risk assessment; system security plan; security assessment report; vulnerability scanning tools and associated configuration documentation; vulnerability scanning results; patch and vulnerability management records; other relevant documents or records].

Test: [*SELECT FROM:* Organizational processes for vulnerability scanning, analysis, remediation, and information sharing; mechanisms supporting or implementing vulnerability scanning, analysis, remediation, and information sharing].

## 3.11.3 Remediate vulnerabilities in accordance with assessments of risk.

MINIMUM ANSWER: Typically, anti-virus and anti-malware security applications cannot only detect but remove and quarantine malicious software. Update documentation accordingly.

This control also addresses "vulnerabilities" that are created by not meeting a specific control within the identified NIST 800-171 families. To address these re-assessment activities, it is normal to update system POAM documentation with explicit reasons any control is not met in full. This should attempt to answer what mitigation solutions are employed? When, by a specific date, the vulnerability will be corrected?

MORE COMPLETE ANSWER: Some additional means to better address this RA control is through other external services that can support ongoing remediation efforts. This could include the C/U 's ISP or Cloud Service Providers. This could also include regular reviews of POAMs by both management and IT support staff personnel, for example, monthly or quarterly.

| ASSESSMENT OBJECTIVE *Determine if:* | | |
|---|---|---|
| **SUB-CTRL** | *DESCRIPTION* | **RECOMMENDED APPROACH** |
| **3.11.3[a]** | *Vulnerabilities are identified.* | NCR |
| **3.11.3[b]** | *Vulnerabilities are remediated in accordance with risk assessments.* | NCR |

**ASSESSMENT METHODS AND CANDIDATE ARTIFACTS FOR REVIEW**

Examine: [*SELECT FROM:* Risk assessment policy; procedures addressing vulnerability scanning; risk assessment; system security plan; security assessment report; vulnerability scanning tools and associated configuration documentation; vulnerability scanning results; patch and vulnerability management records; other relevant documents or records].

Test: [*SELECT FROM:* Organizational processes for vulnerability scanning, analysis, remediation, and information sharing; mechanisms supporting or implementing vulnerability scanning, analysis, remediation, and information sharing].

# SECURITY ASSESSMENT (SA)
## Beginning Continuous Monitoring and Control Reviews

The SA control is about a process that re-assesses the state of all security controls and whether changes have occurred requiring additional mitigations of new risks or threats. The standard is 1/3rd of the controls are to be re-assessed annually. This would require designated IT personnel conduct a SA event of approximately 36-37 controls per year. This should be captured in what is called a **ConMon Plan**. (See Appendix D, *CONTINUOUS MONITORING: A More Detailed Discussion* is an in-depth discussion of the current and future state of Continuous Monitoring and what it may mean to C/U).

**Continuous Monitoring** is a key component of the NIST 800 series cybersecurity protection framework. It is defined as "...maintaining ongoing awareness of information security, vulnerabilities, and threats to support organizational risk management decisions," (NIST Special Publication 800-137, *Information Security Continuous Monitoring (ISCM) for Federal Information Systems and Organizations*, http://nvlpubs.nist.gov/nistpubs/Legacy/SP/nistspecialpublication800-137.pdf ).

---

### *ConMon is a significant guiding principle for the recurring execution of a Security Assessment*

---

**Basic Security Requirements:**

**3.12.1 Periodically assess the security controls in organizational information systems to determine if the controls are effective in their application.**
MINIMUM ANSWER: As described in the opening paragraph, meeting the basic requirements of the Security Assessment control should include the creation of a ConMon Plan and a review of 33% of the controls at least annually.

MORE COMPLETE ANSWER: A more thorough execution could include more than 33% of the controls being reviewed and reassessed; it is suggested to provide the results of annual Security Assessments to government contracting or their designated recipients.

| ASSESSMENT OBJECTIVE *Determine if:* | | |
|---|---|---|
| **SUB-CTRL** | **DESCRIPTION** | **RECOMMENDED APPROACH** |
| **3.12.1[a]** | *The frequency of security control assessments is defined.* | P- 1/3 of the controls should be assessed annually (typical) |
| **3.12.1[b]** | *Security controls are assessed with the defined frequency to determine if the controls are effective in their application.* | P-ConMon Plan will identify "...Security controls ... assessed with ... defined frequency to determine if the controls are effective in their application." |

**ASSESSMENT METHODS AND CANDIDATE ARTIFACTS FOR REVIEW**

Examine: [*SELECT FROM:* Security assessment and authorization policy; procedures addressing security assessment planning; procedures addressing security assessments; security assessment plan; system security plan; other relevant documents or records].

Test: [*SELECT FROM:* Mechanisms supporting security assessment, security assessment plan development, and security assessment reporting].

## 3.12.2 Develop and implement plans of action designed to correct deficiencies and reduce or eliminate vulnerabilities in organizational information systems.

MINIMUM ANSWER: Where the security control is not fully implemented by the C/U or not recognized by the government as being fully compliant, a detailed POAM is necessary; review guidance under the AC control for a more detailed discussion of what is required in preparing a POAM for review.

As described earlier, this should include activities that are meant to answer the control in full or at least leverage other physical and virtual elements of other security controls to reinforce the posture of the control in question. A well-written POAM that is tracked and managed serves as the foundation for a strong risk management process.

> *Cybersecurity is a leadership, not a technical challenge*

MORE COMPLETE ANSWER: Regular reviews by management and IT staff should enhance the C/U's cybersecurity posture. Cybersecurity is not just something that IT security personnel do; it includes the active oversight and review by C/U leadership to ensure effectiveness.

| ASSESSMENT OBJECTIVE *Determine if:* | | |
|---|---|---|
| **SUB-CTRL** | **DESCRIPTION** | **RECOMMENDED APPROACH** |
| **3.12.2[a]** | *Deficiencies and vulnerabilities to be addressed by the plan of action are identified.* | NCR – (The POAM) |

| 3.12.2[b] | A plan of action is developed to correct identified deficiencies and reduce or eliminate identified vulnerabilities. | NCR |
|---|---|---|
| 3.12.2[c] | The plan of action is implemented to correct identified deficiencies and reduce or eliminate identified vulnerabilities. | NCR |

**ASSESSMENT METHODS AND CANDIDATE ARTIFACTS FOR REVIEW**

Examine: [SELECT FROM: Security assessment and authorization policy; procedures addressing plan of action; system security plan; security assessment plan; security assessment report; security assessment evidence; plan of action; other relevant documents or records].

Test: [SELECT FROM: Mechanisms for developing, implementing, and maintaining plan of action].

## 3.12.3 Monitor information system security controls on an ongoing basis to ensure the continued effectiveness of the controls.

MINIMUM ANSWER: This control can be answered in terms of a well-developed and executed ConMon Plan. Describing its purpose and the actions of assigned personnel to accomplish this task will answer this control.

MORE COMPLETE ANSWER: Suggested additional efforts regarding this control could include ad hoc spot checks of controls outside of the annual review process. Identify using the **PPT Model** described in Control 3.6.1 who is responsible for conducting the assessment (people), the workflow to adequately assess the current state of the control (process), and any supporting automation that provides feedback and reporting to management (technology).

## 3.12.4 Develop, document, and periodically update system security plans that describe system boundaries, system environments of operation, how security requirements are implemented, and the relationships with or connections to other systems.

MINIMUM ANSWER: this control requires that the **SSP** is updated regularly. The SSP should at a minimum be reviewed *annually* by designated C/U cybersecurity/IT personnel to ensure its accuracy. The SSP should be specifically updated sooner if there are major changes to the:

- Hardware
- Software
- Network Architecture/Topology

MORE COMPLETE ANSWER: A more complete means to address this control is by addressing in C/U change control boards. These are regular meetings when changes to hardware, software or architecture occur. This should include mechanisms to document the occurrence of application and security patching. An effective procedure should always address changes to the IT system.

| ASSESSMENT OBJECTIVE *Determine if:* | | |
|---|---|---|
| **SUB-CTRL** | *DESCRIPTION* | **RECOMMENDED APPROACH** |
| **3.12.4[a]** | *A system security plan is developed.* | NCR – (The SSP) |
| **3.12.4[b]** | *The system boundary is described and documented in the system security plan.* | NCR (SSP) |
| **3.12.4[c]** | *The system environment of operation is described and documented in the system security plan.* | NCR (SSP) |
| **3.12.4[d]** | *The security requirements identified and approved by the designated authority as non-applicable are identified.* | NCR (SSP) |
| **3.12.4[e]** | *The method of security requirement implementation is described and documented in the system security plan.* | NCR (SSP) |
| **3.12.4[f]** | *The relationship with or connection to other systems is described and documented in the system security plan.* | NCR (SSP) – This is specific to external systems such as telecommunications carriers or other servers (computers) accessed by the local IT environment to meet its mission requirements |
| **3.12.4[g]** | *The frequency to update the system security plan is defined.* | P-The SSP should be updated when major or more specifically, "security relevant" changes happen to the IT environment. |
| **3.12.4[h]** | *System security plan is updated with the defined frequency.* | P-While changes to the SSP should relate to major changes for the purposes of this sub-control we recommend an update at least every 90-180 days depending on the C/U or agencies complexity |

**ASSESSMENT METHODS AND CANDIDATE ARTIFACTS FOR REVIEW**

Examine: [*SELECT FROM:* Security planning policy; procedures addressing system security plan development and implementation; procedures addressing system security plan reviews and updates; enterprise architecture documentation; system security plan; records of system security plan reviews and updates; other relevant documents or records].

Test: [*SELECT FROM:* Organizational processes for system security plan development, review, update, and approval; mechanisms supporting the system security plan].

**Derived Security Requirements:**   None.

# SYSTEM AND COMMUNICATIONS PROTECTION (SC)
## External Communication and Connection Security

The overall risk management strategy is a key in establishing the appropriate technical solutions as well as procedural direction and guidance for the C/U. The core of this security control is it establishes policy based upon applicable federal laws, Executive Orders, directives, regulations, policies, standards, and guidance. This control focuses on information security policy that can reflect the complexity of a C/U and its operation with the government. The procedures should be established for the security of the overall IT architecture and specifically for the components (hardware and software) of the information system.

In this control, many of the prior reinforcing controls can be used in demonstrating to the government a fuller understanding of NIST 800-171 requirements. The apparent repetition of other already developed technical solutions and procedural guides can be used as supporting these controls. However, it is important that C/U procedures are addressed individually—this is for traceability purposes of any potential current or future audit of the C/U 's work by the government; clear and aligned explanations of the controls will make the approval process quicker.

---

## Basic Security Requirements:

**3.13.1 Monitor, control, and protect organizational communications (i.e., information transmitted or received by organizational information systems) at the external boundaries and key internal boundaries of the information systems.**

MINIMUM ANSWER: This control can be answered in the C/U procedure and include, for example, active auditing that checks for unauthorized access, individuals (external) who have had numerous failed logons, and traffic entering the network from "blacklisted" addresses, etc. The C/U should refer to its specific audit procedure as described in more detail under the AU control.

MORE COMPLETE ANSWER: This control could be better met as formerly discussed by using "smart" firewalls and advanced SIEM solutions. While costlier and requiring greater technical experience, C/U leadership should consider. These solutions while not necessarily cost effective for the current state of the C/U, it should be considered as part of any future architectural change effort. Any planning efforts should consider current and future technology purchases meant to enhance the cybersecurity posture of the C/U. See Appendix D for a broader description of SIEM technologies and how they may become part of the IT infrastructure.

| ASSESSMENT OBJECTIVE *Determine if:* | | |
|---|---|---|
| **SUB-CTRL** | *DESCRIPTION* | **RECOMMENDED APPROACH** |
| **3.13.1[a]** | *The external system boundary is defined.* | P/SSP-The "external system" boundary here is specific to firewalls and DMZ's. **This is part of the SSP.** This control also addresses protections, and this is only meant to identify where the "security boundary" is defined and known. |
| **3.13.1[b]** | *Key internal system boundaries are defined.* | SSP |
| **3.13.1[c]** | *Communications are monitored at the external system boundary.* | P- *"Communications are monitored at the external system boundary"* |
| **3.13.1[d]** | *Communications are monitored at key internal boundaries.* | P- *"Communications are monitored at key internal boundaries"* |
| **3.13.1[e]** | *Communications are controlled at the external system boundary.* | P- *"Communications are controlled at the external system boundary"* |
| **3.13.1[f]** | *Communications are controlled at key internal boundaries.* | P- *"Communications are controlled at key internal boundaries"* |
| **3.13.1[g]** | *Communications are protected at the external system boundary.* | P- *"Communications are protected at the external system boundary"* |
| **3.13.1[h]** | *Communications are protected at key internal boundaries.* | P- *"Communications are protected at key internal boundaries"*<br><br>■ **This is where NIST 800-171A gets "granular" to a significant degree.** |

**ASSESSMENT METHODS AND CANDIDATE ARTIFACTS FOR REVIEW**

Examine: [*SELECT FROM:* System and communications protection policy; procedures addressing boundary protection; system security plan; list of key internal boundaries of the system; system design documentation; boundary protection hardware and software; enterprise security architecture documentation; system audit logs and records; system configuration settings and associated documentation; other relevant documents or records].

Test: [*SELECT FROM:* Mechanisms implementing boundary protection capability].

## 3.13.2 Employ architectural designs, software development techniques, and systems engineering principles that promote effective information security within organizational information systems.

MINIMUM/MORE COMPLETE ANSWER: Describing effective security architectural design measures can be as simple as the employment of a properly configured firewall or 2FA/MFA utilized by the C/U. It is highly likely that the average C/U seeking contracts with the government will be specifically concerned with basic and secure architectures.

Other **mitigation** elements that can be described for this control may include physical security measures (e.g., a 24-hour guard force, reinforced fire doors, and cameras) or blacklist measures that prevent unauthorized applications from executing in the C/U network. See Control 3.13.10 for how 2FA operates internal or external to a C/U 's network.

| ASSESSMENT OBJECTIVE *Determine if:* | | |
|---|---|---|
| **SUB-CTRL** | *DESCRIPTION* | **RECOMMENDED APPROACH** |
| **3.13.2[a]** | *Architectural designs that promote effective information security are identified.* | NCR/SSP-This includes firewalls, Intrusion Protection/Detection devices, etc. |
| **3.13.2[b]** | *Software development techniques that promote effective information security are identified.* | P- This requires that software development follows secure coding, scripting, etc., best practices, directions, and guidelines such as for DOD, Application Security Development (APPSECDEV) guidance. |
| **3.13.2[c]** | *Systems engineering principles that promote effective information security are identified.* | P- This requires that systems engineering follows secure engineering best practices. |
| **3.13.2[d]** | *Identified architectural designs that promote effective information security are employed.* | P- This requires that IT architecture and design follow secure engineering best practices. |
| **3.13.2[e]** | *Identified software development techniques that promote effective information security are employed.* | P- (See 3.13.2[b]) <br>■ Some of these control requirements may be reflected with third-party developers in the form of a contract. |
| **3.13.2[f]** | *Identified systems engineering principles that promote effective information security are employed.* | P- (See 3.13.2[c]) <br>■ Some of these control requirements may be reflected with third-party developers in the form of a contract. |

**ASSESSMENT METHODS AND CANDIDATE ARTIFACTS FOR REVIEW**

Examine: [*SELECT FROM:* Security planning policy; procedures addressing system security plan development and implementation; procedures addressing system security plan reviews and updates; enterprise architecture documentation; system security plan; records of system security plan reviews and updates; system and communications protection policy; procedures addressing security engineering principles used in the specification, design, development, implementation, and modification of the system; security architecture documentation; security requirements and specifications for the system; system design documentation; system configuration settings and associated documentation;  other relevant documents or records].

Test: [*SELECT FROM:* Organizational processes for system security plan development, review, update, and approval; mechanisms supporting the system security plan; processes for applying security engineering principles in system specification, design, development, implementation, and modification; automated mechanisms supporting the application of security engineering principles in information system specification, design, development, implementation, and modification].

**Derived Security Requirements:**

## 3.13.3 Separate user functionality from information system management functionality.

MINIMUM ANSWER:  The policy should not allow privileged users to use the same credentials to access their user (e.g., email and Internet searches) and privileged user accesses.  This separation of access is a basic network security principle and is intended to hamper both insider and external threats.  (A suggested review of a similar control is Control 3.1.4, and its discussion of the **segregation of duties** principle for comparison.)

MORE COMPLETE ANSWER: There are technical solutions to automate this process.  The product, for example, CyberArk ® is used in many parts of the federal government to track and account for privileged user activity that is easily auditable. The ability to oversee especially privileged user activity should be readily audited and reviewed by senior C/U cybersecurity representatives.

| ASSESSMENT OBJECTIVE *Determine if:* | | |
|---|---|---|
| **SUB-CTRL** | *DESCRIPTION* | **RECOMMENDED APPROACH** |
| **3.13.3[a]** | *User functionality is identified.* | NCR |
| **3.13.3[b]** | *System management functionality is identified.* | NCR (This addresses functionality such as System, Database Administrators, etc.) |
| **3.13.3[c]** | *User functionality is separated from system management functionality.* | NCR |

**POTENTIAL ASSESSMENT METHODS AND CANDIDATE ARTIFACTS FOR REVIEW**
Examine: [*SELECT FROM:* System and communications protection policy; procedures addressing application partitioning; system design documentation; system configuration settings and associated documentation; system security plan; system audit logs and records; other relevant documents or records].
Test: [*SELECT FROM:* Separation of user functionality from system management functionality].

## 3.13.4 Prevent unauthorized and unintended information transfer via shared system resources.

MINIMUM ANSWER: **Peer-to-peer** networking is not authorized within many parts of the government, and it is strongly suggested the C/U 's network also forbids its use.  This is typically part of the AUP and should be enforceable to prevent, e.g., insider threat opportunities or used by external hackers to gain unauthorized access using legitimate employee security credentials.

MORE COMPLETE ANSWER: Suggest that this is part of the normal audit activity by designated IT personnel. They could be reviewing audit logs for unauthorized connections to include peer-to-peer networking.

### 3.13.5 Implement subnetworks for publicly accessible system components that are physically or logically separated from internal networks.

MINIMUM/MORE COMPLETE ANSWER: The simplest answer is that subnetworks reduce an intruder's ability to effectively exploit C/U network addresses. Have IT personnel establish subnetworks specifically for the email and webservers that are in the external Demilitarized Zone (DMZ) of the C/U 's security boundary; see Control 3.14.2 for the location of a DMZ relative to the C/U 's network. Some companies maintain external database servers; ensure they too have established subnetwork addresses.

| ASSESSMENT OBJECTIVE *Determine if:* | | |
|---|---|---|
| **SUB-CTRL** | *DESCRIPTION* | **RECOMMENDED APPROACH** |
| **3.13.5[a]** | *Publicly accessible system components are identified.* | NCR (Also should be part of SSP) |
| **3.13.5[b]** | *Subnetworks for publicly accessible system components are physically or logically separated from internal networks.* | NCR |

**ASSESSMENT METHODS AND CANDIDATE ARTIFACTS FOR REVIEW**

Examine: [*SELECT FROM:* System and communications protection policy; procedures addressing boundary protection; system security plan; list of key internal boundaries of the system; system design documentation; boundary protection hardware and software; system configuration settings and associated documentation; enterprise security architecture documentation; system audit logs and records; other relevant documents or records].

Test: [*SELECT FROM:* Mechanisms implementing boundary protection capability].

### 3.13.6 Deny network communications traffic by default and allow network communications traffic by exception (i.e., deny all, permit by exception).

MINIMUM/MORE COMPLETE ANSWER: Like Control 3.4.8, this control can be selected by IT personnel. This is a technical control that should also be captured in the procedure document. These network settings are typically set at the firewall and involve **whitelisting** (only permitting access by exception) and **blacklisting** (from non-authorized Internet addresses) everyone else to enter the network. (Also, review Control 3.14.2.)

| ASSESSMENT OBJECTIVE *Determine if:* | | |
|---|---|---|
| **SUB-CTRL** | *DESCRIPTION* | **RECOMMENDED APPROACH** |
| **3.13.6[a]** | *Network communications traffic is denied by default.* | NCR |
| **3.13.6[b]** | *Network communications traffic is allowed by exception.* | NCR |

**ASSESSMENT METHODS AND CANDIDATE ARTIFACTS FOR REVIEW**

Examine: *[SELECT FROM: System and communications protection policy; procedures addressing boundary protection; system security plan; system design documentation; system configuration settings and associated documentation; system audit logs and records; other relevant documents or records].*

Test: *[SELECT FROM: Mechanisms implementing traffic management at managed interfaces].*

## 3.13.7 Prevent remote devices from simultaneously establishing non-remote connections with the information system and communicating via some other connection to resources in external networks.

MINIMUM/MORE COMPLETE ANSWER: If a teleworking employee uses their remote device (i.e., notebook computer), and then connects to a non-remote (external) connection, it allows for an unauthorized external connection to exist; this provides a potential hacker with the ability to enter the network using the authorized employee's credentials.

It is critical that the C/U require employees to use their VPN connection and blocks any unsecure connections from accessing internal systems or applications. IT personnel need to ensure these settings are properly configured and are part of the C/U cybersecurity procedure documentation.

## 3.13.8 Implement cryptographic mechanisms to prevent unauthorized disclosure of CUI during transmission unless otherwise protected by alternative physical safeguards.

MINIMUM ANSWER: Remember, this control is about external communications from the network and its system boundary. This is a DIT issue and is protected by the cryptographic solutions discussed earlier; see Control 3.1.3. Documentation should reflect the type and level of protection of data transmitted. Any additional protections such as a VPN, a secure circuit/dedicated circuit provided by a commercially contracted carrier may afford more security for C/U data transmissions.

MORE COMPLETE ANSWER: Better levels of protection could be addressed regarding defense in depth which is a current operational philosophy supported by the government; additional layers of security provide additional defense. (See the "Defense-in-Depth" diagram at Control 3.14.2).

| ASSESSMENT OBJECTIVE *Determine if:* | | |
|---|---|---|
| **SUB-CTRL** | *DESCRIPTION* | **RECOMMENDED APPROACH** |
| **3.13.8[a]** | *Cryptographic mechanisms intended to prevent unauthorized disclosure of CUI are identified.* | NCR |
| **3.13.8[b]** | *Alternative physical safeguards intended to prevent unauthorized disclosure of CUI are identified.* | NCR |
| **3.13.8[c]** | *Either cryptographic mechanisms or alternative physical safeguards are implemented to prevent unauthorized disclosure of CUI during transmission.* | NCR |

**POTENTIAL ASSESSMENT METHODS AND CANDIDATE ARTIFACTS FOR REVIEW**

Examine: [*SELECT FROM:* System and communications protection policy; procedures addressing transmission confidentiality and integrity; system security plan; system design documentation; system configuration settings and associated documentation; system audit logs and records; other relevant documents or records].

Test: [*SELECT FROM:* Cryptographic mechanisms or mechanisms supporting or implementing transmission confidentiality; organizational processes for defining and implementing alternative physical safeguards].

## 3.13.9 Terminate network connections associated with communications sessions at the end of the sessions or after a defined period of inactivity.

MINIMUM ANSWER: This was addressed in the AC control specific to the complete termination of a session. Sessions of suggested importance would be those such as to the financial, HR, or other key computer server systems housing defined CUI/CDI. It is recommended that the procedure is updated specifically to this control re-using language provided by any response to the control(s) discussing the termination of a network connection.

MORE COMPLETE ANSWER: Audit of sessions that have timed-out can strengthen this control. SA's and IT staff can determine from audit logs that the prescribed time-out period was met and enforced. Provide a sampling to any inspector as part of the final packet.

| ASSESSMENT OBJECTIVE *Determine if:* | | |
|---|---|---|
| **SUB-CTRL** | *DESCRIPTION* | **RECOMMENDED APPROACH** |
| **3.13.9[a]** | *A period of inactivity to terminate network connections associated with communications sessions is defined.* | NCR |
| **3.13.9[b]** | *Network connections associated with communications sessions are terminated at the end of the sessions.* | NCR |

| 3.13.9[c] | Network connections associated with communications sessions are terminated after the defined period of inactivity. | NCR |
|---|---|---|

**ASSESSMENT METHODS AND CANDIDATE ARTIFACTS FOR REVIEW**

Examine: [SELECT FROM: System and communications protection policy; procedures addressing network disconnect; system design documentation; system security plan; system configuration settings and associated documentation; system audit logs and records; other relevant documents or records].

Test: [SELECT FROM: Mechanisms supporting or implementing network disconnect capability].

## 3.13.10 Establish and manage cryptographic keys for cryptography employed in the information system.

MINIMUM ANSWER: There are two major scenarios likely to occur:

1. Use of commercial cryptographic programs that resides within the C/U 's architecture or is provided by an external "managed service" provider are the most likely scenarios. The keys will be maintained and secured by the cryptographic application. The C/U are establishing some form of 2FA solution. The public key would be secured somewhere else in the architecture, and the private key, that of the employee, would reside on a token such as CAC card or another key device.

2. Using a 2FA solution with a CAC, Personal Identity Verification (PIV) card or "token" such as those produced by RSA ® is likely if the government authorizes the exchange of security keys on its systems with that of the C/U. This requires a Certificate Authority (CA) usually outside the local network either managed by the government or another trusted commercial entity with the capability to support "asymmetric" 2FA.

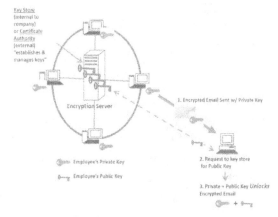

**Two-factor Authentication (2FA) – Asymmetric Cryptography Basic Description**

Whichever solution is used, ensure compatibility with government systems and other companies' as part of its normal operations. ***All transmittal of CUI/CDI data is required to be encrypted.***

MORE COMPLETE ANSWER: Any greater ability to secure and protect the **key store** within the C/U or through defined SLA's with outside service providers is important. Ensure they have safeguards in place to protect unauthorized access to its system as well; they may use stronger encryption methods, but ensure they are recognized by the government and are Federal Information Processing Standards (FIPS 140-2) compliant. (See Control 3.13.11 for identifying FIPS 140-2 solutions).

| ASSESSMENT OBJECTIVE *Determine if:* | | |
|---|---|---|
| **SUB-CTRL** | *DESCRIPTION* | **RECOMMENDED APPROACH** |
| **3.13.10[a]** | *Cryptographic keys are established whenever cryptography is employed.* | NCR |
| **3.13.10[b]** | *Cryptographic keys are managed whenever cryptography is employed.* | NCR |

**ASSESSMENT METHODS AND CANDIDATE ARTIFACTS FOR REVIEW**
Examine: [*SELECT FROM:* System and communications protection policy; procedures addressing cryptographic key establishment and management; system security plan; system design documentation; cryptographic mechanisms; system configuration settings and associated documentation; system audit logs and records; other relevant documents or records].
Test: [*SELECT FROM:* Mechanisms supporting or implementing cryptographic key establishment and management].

---

## External Certification Authority Program (ECA)

In the case of DOD, the ECA program affords C/U the ability to interface with its 2FA infrastructure. The ECA supports the issuing of DoD-approved certificates to industry partners and other external third-party entities and organizations. The ECA program is designed to provide the mechanism for vendors to securely communicate with the DoD and authenticate to DoD Information Systems. It is expected to be further leveraged by other federal agencies as NIST 800-171 requirements expand the DOD.

For new vendors the following instructions should be helpful when the ECA requirement becomes mandatory. To obtain a Public Key Infrastructure (PKI) ECA Medium Assurance Certificate (MAC), it will be most likely be obtained by two major current vendors. The two vendors are: Either through the **Operational Research Consultants, Inc. (ORC)** at https://eca.orc.com/ or IdenTrust at http://www.identrust.com/certificates/eca/index.html). The certificate will come in three forms: Software (browser based), token (preloaded USB device), or hardware (CAC card loaded).

The cost ranges from $100-$300 and are good from one to three years depending on the selected option. When visiting these sites ensure that the correct certificate is chosen. Select the "ECA/Identity certificate." On the IdenTrust web site look for the Medium Assurance Certificate.

The process will take from one to two weeks to receive the certificate. The certificate will be provided by email with the instructions on how to download the certificate. Once the certificate is received, contact the Contract Office to determine what help desk will need to be contacted to request account establishment on the respective federal IT infrastructure. It will typically require at least 30 minutes to 1 hour to create the account but expect longer with non-DOD federal agencies.

**IdenTrust DOD ECA Program Site**

---

## 3.13.11 Employ FIPS-validated cryptography when used to protect the confidentiality of CUI.

MINIMUM/MORE COMPLETE ANSWER:  The C/U need to confirm that its encryption applications are FIPS 140-2 compliant.  It can easily be verified at the website below:

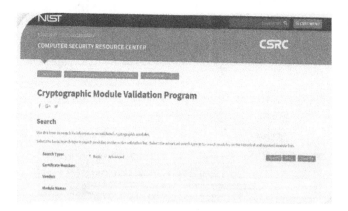

**Official NIST site to confirm FIPS 140-2 cryptographic compliance**
(https://csrc.nist.gov/projects/cryptographic-module-validation-program/validated-modules/search)

## 3.13.12 Prohibit remote activation of collaborative computing devices and provide indication of devices in use to users present at the device.

MINIMUM ANSWER: Collaborative computing devices include, for example, "networked whiteboards, cameras, and microphones." The intent is to prevent these devices being used by intruders to conduct reconnaissance of a network.

This can be prevented by changes in registry settings that only authorized IT personnel with privileged access can change. Furthermore, if these items are active, visible lighting or audible alerts, should be considered to notify IT and security personnel. Policy should require that individuals do not change these settings to include privileged users. Any change should only be approved by exception and require a privileged user who is authorized to make such changes.

MORE COMPLETE ANSWER: Auditing and SIEM solutions could be configured to ensure these settings are not tampered with. See Control 3.3.2 for further discussion of this topic area.

| ASSESSMENT OBJECTIVE *Determine if:* | | |
|---|---|---|
| **SUB-CTRL** | *DESCRIPTION* | **RECOMMENDED APPROACH** |
| **3.13.12[a]** | *Collaborative computing devices are identified.* | NCR |
| **3.13.12[b]** | *Collaborative computing devices provide indication to users of devices in use.* | NCR |
| **3.13.12[c]** | *Remote activation of collaborative computing devices is prohibited.* | P - *"Remote activation of collaborative computing devices is prohibited"* |

**ASSESSMENT METHODS AND CANDIDATE ARTIFACTS FOR REVIEW**

<u>Examine</u>: [*SELECT FROM*: System and communications protection policy; procedures addressing collaborative computing; access control policy and procedures; system security plan; system design documentation; system audit logs and records; system configuration settings and associated documentation; other relevant documents or records].

<u>Test</u>: [*SELECT FROM*: Mechanisms supporting or implementing management of remote activation of collaborative computing devices; mechanisms providing an indication of use of collaborative computing devices].

## 3.13.13 Control and monitor the use of mobile code.

MINIMUM/MORE COMPLETE ANSWER:  Mobile code is mainly part of Internet-capable C/U phones.  The C/U's phone carrier can limit the types and kinds of mobile applications that reside on employee phones.  Most applications are usually required to meet secure industry development standards.  It is best to confirm with the C/U's carrier how mobile code apps are secured and restrict employees to a set number of approved mobile apps.  Define in the C/U procedures the base applications provided to each employee, and the process for work specific applications that other specialists in the C/U require.

**ASSESSMENT OBJECTIVE** *Determine if:*

| SUB-CTRL | DESCRIPTION | RECOMMENDED APPROACH |
|---|---|---|
| 3.13.13[a] | Use of mobile code is controlled. | P – "Use of mobile code is controlled." (Restricted through a carrier and must be approved by the C/U authorized representative before accessible by employees). |
| 3.13.13[b] | Use of mobile code is monitored. | P – "Use of mobile code is monitored." (Reports provided on an established/contractual basis). |

**ASSESSMENT METHODS AND CANDIDATE ARTIFACTS FOR REVIEW**

<u>Examine</u>: [*SELECT FROM*: System and communications protection policy; procedures addressing mobile code; mobile code usage restrictions, mobile code implementation policy and procedures; system audit logs and records; system security plan; list of acceptable mobile code and mobile code technologies; list of unacceptable mobile code and mobile technologies; authorization records; system monitoring records; system audit logs and records; other relevant documents or records].

<u>Test</u>: [*SELECT FROM*: Organizational process for controlling, authorizing, monitoring, and restricting mobile code; mechanisms supporting or implementing the management of mobile code; mechanisms supporting or implementing the monitoring of mobile code].

## 3.13.14 Control and monitor the use of Voice over Internet Protocol (VoIP) technologies.

MINIMUM ANSWER: The most likely current place VOIP would exist is the C/U's phone service.  Ensure with the phone carrier that their VOIP services are secure and what level of security is used to protect C/U communications.  Furthermore, identify any contract information that provides details about the provided security.

MORE COMPLETE ANSWER: Verify what monitoring services and network protection (from malware, viruses, etc.) are part of the current service plan.  If necessary, determine whether both the control and monitoring are included or extra services.  If not fully included, consider formulating a POAM.

| ASSESSMENT OBJECTIVE *Determine if:* | | |
|---|---|---|
| **SUB-CTRL** | **DESCRIPTION** | **RECOMMENDED APPROACH** |
| **3.13.14[a]** | *Use of Voice over Internet Protocol (VoIP) technologies is controlled.* | NCR (See sub-control 3.13.13[a] for a similar discussion) |
| **3.13.14[b]** | *Use of Voice over Internet Protocol (VoIP) technologies is monitored.* | NCR |

**ASSESSMENT METHODS AND CANDIDATE ARTIFACTS FOR REVIEW**
Examine: [*SELECT FROM:* System and communications protection policy; procedures addressing VoIP; VoIP usage restrictions; VoIP implementation guidance; system security plan; system design documentation; system audit logs and records; system configuration settings and associated documentation; system monitoring records; other relevant documents or records].

Test: [*SELECT FROM:* Organizational process for authorizing, monitoring, and controlling VoIP; mechanisms supporting or implementing authorizing, monitoring, and controlling VoIP].

## 3.13.15 Protect the authenticity of communications sessions.

MINIMUM/ MORE COMPLETE ANSWER: This control addresses communications' protection and establishes confidence that the session is authentic; it ensures the identity of the individual and the information being transmitted. Authenticity protection includes, for example, protecting against session hijacking or insertion of false information.

This can be resolved by some form, hard or soft token MFA/2FA, solution. It will ensure the identity and FIPS 140-2 encryption to prevent data manipulation.  See Control 3.5.2 for further discussion.  While these are not absolute solutions, they greatly demonstrate more certainty that the communications are authentic.

## 3.13.16 Protect the confidentiality of CUI at rest.

MINIMUM ANSWER:  This is a DAR issue, and as discussed earlier, it is a government requirement.  Ensure the proper software package is procured that meets FIPS 140-2 standards. (See Control 3.13.11 for NIST's website information).

MORE COMPLETE ANSWER: If using a CSP, ensure it is using government accepted FIPS 140-2 standards; it will make authorization simpler. And, a reminder, if the C/U cannot use FIPS 140-2 solutions, ensures an effective POAM is developed that addresses why it cannot be currently implemented and when the C/U is prepared to implement the control. *When will the C/U be compliant?*

# SYSTEM AND INFORMATION INTEGRITY (SI)
## Anti-virus and Anti-Malware

This control family is about maintaining the integrity of data within the C/U 's system security boundary.  It primarily defended by active measures such as anti-virus and malware protection. This control addresses the establishment of procedures for effective implementation of the security controls. Cybersecurity policies and procedures may include Information Security (INFOSEC) policies.  C/U risk management strategy is a key factor in establishing decisive system protections.

---

**Basic Security Requirements:**

**3.14.1 Identify, report, and correct information and information system flaws in a timely manner.**
MINIMUM ANSWER: This control addresses what are considered security-relevant flaws.  These would include, for example, software patches, hotfixes, anti-virus and anti-malware signatures.

Typically, network Operating Systems can check with manufacturers via the Internet for updated, e.g., "security patches" in near-real time.  It is important to allow patches from the authorized manufacturers and sources be updated as soon as possible.  They usually are designed to fix bugs and minor through major security vulnerabilities.  The sooner the system is updated, the better.  Ensure a process, such as checks by IT personnel at least twice a day.  Many systems will allow for automated "pushes" to the network.  Ensure that documented processes account for review by IT personnel to "audit" known pushes by only authorized sources.

---

**Major Security Events/Zero-Day Attacks**: There are times that the federal government becomes aware of **zero-day attacks**.  These are attacks where there is no current security patch and sometimes requires other actions by government supported organizations and C/U s; be aware of these events from DOD and Department of Homeland Security (DHS) alerts. These will require near-immediate action.  Furthermore, the government may direct everyone, including NIST 800-171 authorized C/U, report their status to the Contract Officer by an established deadline.

---

MORE COMPLETE ANSWER:  Ensure that designated IT personnel are aware of and are monitoring the active vulnerabilities sites from both DOD and DHS.  An active process to verify the current state of threats against the government is an excellent means to establish a C/U 's due diligence in this area.

DHS's United States Computer Emergency Readiness Team (US-CERT) has the latest information on vulnerabilities to include zero-day updates.  It is also recommended that designated IT personnel sign up for the Rich Site Summary (RSS) data feeds by the selecting the symbol to the left.  The address for the overall site is: https://www.us-cert.gov/ncas/current-activity

| ASSESSMENT OBJECTIVE *Determine if:* | | |
|---|---|---|
| **SUB-CTRL** | *DESCRIPTION* | **RECOMMENDED APPROACH** |
| **3.14.1[a]** | *The time within which to identify system flaws is specified.* | P – Suggested: "Upon notification from X or upon recognition that software patches or hotfixes are out of date; anti-virus and anti-malware signatures are not current, etc. |
| **3.14.1[b]** | *System flaws are identified within the specified time frame.* | P- This at a minimum should be upon recognition and a process that is in-place to identify when reviews should occur, typically, weekly. |
| **3.14.1[c]** | *The time within which to report system flaws is specified.* | P – (See above) |
| **3.14.1[d]** | *System flaws are reported within the specified time frame.* | P – (See above) |
| **3.14.1[e]** | *The time within which to correct system flaws is specified.* | P- Flaws should be addressed immediately or within 24 hours, typically.  Where a patch, for example, has a negative effect on operations there needs to be roll-back procedures.  This should then require a POAM be documented with a possible waiver if the change is too negative. |
| **3.14.1[f]** | *System flaws are corrected within the specified time frame.* | P – (See 4.14.1[f]) |

## 3.14.2 Provide protection from malicious code at appropriate locations within organizational information systems.

MINIMUM ANSWER: Protecting the network from malicious code is typically through both active anti-virus and malware protection applications or services. Ensure if additional protections provided by the C/U's commercial ISP are included in any artifact submission.

MORE COMPLETE ANSWER: Any additional protections could be provided by "smart" firewalls, routers, and switches. Certain commercial devices provide extra defenses.

**Smart Firewalls.** Smart firewalls include standard protection capabilities. Additionally, firewalls specifically, can afford whitelisting and blacklisting protections.

- **Whitelisting** can be used only to allow authorized outside users on an internal Access Control List (ACL). The ACL needs to be managed actively to ensure that legitimate organizations can communicate through the C/U's firewall. The external interested C/U or organizations can still communicate with the C/U for some services like the C/U web site and email system that resides in what is termed the Demilitarized Zone (DMZ). Whitelisting is typically implemented at the firewall. See Diagram below.

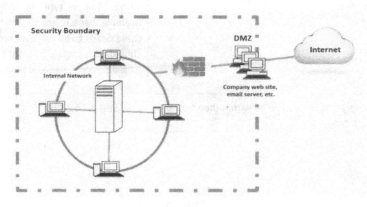

**Basic C/U Network View**

- **Blacklisting** is used to block known "bad guys." There are companies and the government that can provide lists of known malicious sites based upon their Internet address. Blacklists require continuous management to be most effective.

Both solutions are not guaranteed. While they afford additional means to slow hackers and nation-state intruders, they are not total solutions. Therefore, the government, and much of the cybersecurity community, strongly supports the principle of **defense in depth** where other technological solutions help to reinforce the protections because of security programming flaws inadvertently created by software developers and the constant challenge of hackers exploiting various areas of modern IT architectures to conduct their nefarious actions.

**The Principle of Defense in Depth**

| ASSESSMENT OBJECTIVE *Determine if:* | | |
|---|---|---|
| **SUB-CTRL** | *DESCRIPTION* | **RECOMMENDED APPROACH** |
| **3.14.2[a]** | *Designated locations for malicious code protection are identified.* | P/SSP – Should identify the application and mechanisms within the architecture devoted to malicious code identification. |
| **3.14.2[b]** | *Protection from malicious code at designated locations is provided.* | P/SSP – (Same as 3.14.2[a]) |

## 3.14.3 Monitor information system security alerts and advisories and take appropriate actions in response.

MINIMUM ANSWER: This SI control can be best met through auditing. This can be met by using applications (such as anti-virus) or tools embedded within the architecture. These should include Intrusion Detection capabilities, network packet capture tools such as Wireshark ®, or audit logs. The process and associated actions should include recognition and notification to senior management. Management should ensure developed processes define when an event is raised to a level of a notifiable incident to the government.

MORE COMPLETE ANSWER: A more-complete solution could use other advanced toolsets based on the education and experience of the IT support staff. These could include malicious code protection software (such as found in more advanced anti-malware solutions). Consideration should always include the overall ROI for the investment in such tools.

If the C/U can only implement minor portions of the control and has the planned intent to invest in improved tools in the future, it is best to develop a well-defined POAM with achievable milestones for the C/U to pursue. It will demonstrate to the US government a commitment to improving cybersecurity vice ignoring other technical methods to reduce the risk to the C/U and its associated CUI/CDI.

| ASSESSMENT OBJECTIVE *Determine if:* | | |
|---|---|---|
| **SUB-CTRL** | *DESCRIPTION* | **RECOMMENDED APPROACH** |
| **3.14.3[a]** | *Response actions to system security alerts and advisories are identified.* | P – This would align with the Incident Response Plan (IRP); (See IR 3.6 Controls) |
| **3.14.3[b]** | *System security alerts and advisories are monitored.* | P – This would identify who monitors; small companies may include SA's and larger companies with use their Security Operations Center (SOC) watch personnel |

| 3.14.3[c] | Actions in response to system security alerts and advisories are taken. | P – Part of IRP and designated personnel. |
|---|---|---|

**POTENTIAL ASSESSMENT METHODS AND CANDIDATE ARTIFACTS FOR REVIEW**

Examine: [SELECT FROM: System and information integrity policy; procedures addressing security alerts, advisories, and directives; system security plan; records of security alerts and advisories; other relevant documents or records].

Test: [SELECT FROM: Organizational processes for defining, receiving, generating, disseminating, and complying with security alerts, advisories, and directives; mechanisms supporting or implementing definition, receipt, generation, and dissemination of security alerts, advisories, and directives; mechanisms supporting or implementing security directives].

**Derived Security Requirements:**

## 3.14.4 Update malicious code protection mechanisms when new releases are available.

MINIMUM/COMPLETE ANSWER: This is usually easily resolved through ongoing software license agreements with vendors for malicious code internal programs or external contracted support services. Assuming a new version is made available during the active period of the license, updates are typically free; document the C/U 's procedure for maintaining not only current but legal versions of malicious code detection and prevention software or services.

## 3.14.5 Perform periodic scans of the information system and real-time scans of files from external sources as files are downloaded, opened, or executed.

MINIMUM ANSWER: Many of the solutions already discussed afford real-time scanning of files and traffic as they traverse the network. Scanning of files should always be conducted from external downloads for both viruses and malware. Ensure the technical policy settings are always set to conduct real-time scans of the network, endpoints (i.e., work computers both internal and used by teleworking employees), and files entering the network by the appropriate tools to ensure network operation and security.

MORE COMPLETE ANSWER: Require IT personnel to regularly check that real-time scanning has not been changed accidentally or on purpose. It is important to be aware that potential intruders will attempt to shut down any security features such as active scanning. Train IT personnel to manually check at least weekly and alert management if the changes are suspicious. Identifying possible entry into the C/U 's data is a function of the SI as well as a major component of the AU control family.

| ASSESSMENT OBJECTIVE *Determine if:* | | |
|---|---|---|
| **SUB-CTRL** | *DESCRIPTION* | **RECOMMENDED APPROACH** |
| **3.14.5[a]** | *The frequency for malicious code scans is defined.* | NCR – Recommended: real-time using approved malware detection software; otherwise, at least daily for smaller operations (not recommended until tool is purchased and deployed) |
| **3.14.5[b]** | *Malicious code scans are performed with the defined frequency.* | NCR |
| **3.14.5[c]** | *Real-time malicious code scans of files from external sources as files are downloaded, opened, or executed are performed.* | NCR |

**ASSESSMENT METHODS AND CANDIDATE ARTIFACTS FOR REVIEW**

Examine: [*SELECT FROM:* System and information integrity policy; configuration management policy and procedures; procedures addressing malicious code protection; malicious code protection mechanisms; records of malicious code protection updates; system security plan; system design documentation; system configuration settings and associated documentation; scan results from malicious code protection mechanisms; record of actions initiated by malicious code protection mechanisms in response to malicious code detection; system audit logs and records; other relevant documents or records].

Test: [*SELECT FROM:* Organizational processes for employing, updating, and configuring malicious code protection mechanisms; organizational process for addressing false positives and resulting potential impact; mechanisms supporting or implementing malicious code protection mechanisms (including updates and configurations); mechanisms supporting or implementing malicious code scanning and subsequent actions].

## 3.14.6 Monitor the information system including inbound and outbound communications traffic, to detect attacks and indicators of potential attacks.

MINIMUM ANSWER: As discussed, anti-virus and malware provide some level of checking of inbound and outbound traffic. Document both manual and automated means to ensure traffic is monitored.

Procedures should identify the people who will conduct the regular review, the process that ensures proper oversight is in place to identify violations of this control, and what technologies are being used to protect inbound and outbound traffic from attack. (See Control 3.6.1 for discussion about the PPT Model, and its application to address security controls).

MORE COMPLETE ANSWER: This could also identify commercial ISP's supporting the C/U with "trusted" connections to the Internet. Refer to provided SLA's and contract information for government review.

| ASSESSMENT OBJECTIVE *Determine if:* | | |
|---|---|---|
| **SUB-CTRL** | **DESCRIPTION** | **RECOMMENDED APPROACH** |
| **3.14.6[a]** | *The system is monitored to detect attacks and indicators of potential attacks.* | NCR |
| **3.14.6[b]** | *Inbound communications traffic is monitored to detect attacks and indicators of potential attacks.* | NCR |
| **3.14.6[c]** | *Outbound communications traffic is monitored to detect attacks and indicators of potential attacks.* | NCR |

**ASSESSMENT METHODS AND CANDIDATE ARTIFACTS FOR REVIEW**

Examine: [*SELECT FROM:* System and information integrity policy; procedures addressing system monitoring tools and techniques; continuous monitoring strategy; system and information integrity policy; procedures addressing system monitoring tools and techniques; facility diagram or layout; system security plan; system monitoring tools and techniques documentation; system design documentation; locations within system where monitoring devices are deployed; system protocols; system configuration settings and associated documentation; system audit logs and records; other relevant documents or records].

Test: [*SELECT FROM:* Organizational processes for system monitoring; mechanisms supporting or implementing intrusion detection capability and system monitoring; mechanisms supporting or implementing system monitoring capability; organizational processes for intrusion detection and system monitoring; mechanisms supporting or implementing the monitoring of inbound and outbound communications traffic].

## 3.14.7 Identify unauthorized use of the information system.

MINIMUM ANSWER: This is met through active and regular auditing of, for example, systems, applications, intrusion detections, and firewall logs. It is important to recognize that there may be limitations for the IT staff to properly and adequately review all available logs created by the C/U's IT network. It is best to identify the critical logs to review regularly and any secondary logs as time permits. Avoid trying to review all available system logs; there are many. Also, determine the level of effort, required processing time, ability, and training of the C/U's' IT support staff.

MORE COMPLETE ANSWER: In addition to the above, consider third-party companies that can provide a monitoring service of the network. While these may be expensive, it will depend on the C/U, its mission, and the critically of the data. This solution will require a well-developed SLA's with appropriate oversight to ensure the C/U receive the Quality of Service (QOS) the C/U needs.

| ASSESSMENT OBJECTIVE *Determine if:* | | |
|---|---|---|
| **SUB-CTRL** | *DESCRIPTION* | **RECOMMENDED APPROACH** |
| **3.14.7[a]** | *Authorized use of the system is defined.* | NCR |
| **3.14.7[b]** | *Unauthorized use of the system is identified.* | NCR |

**ASSESSMENT METHODS AND CANDIDATE ARTIFACTS FOR REVIEW**

Examine: [SELECT FROM: Continuous monitoring strategy; system and information integrity policy; procedures addressing system monitoring tools and techniques; facility diagram/layout; system security plan; system design documentation; system monitoring tools and techniques documentation; locations within system where monitoring devices are deployed; system configuration settings and associated documentation; other relevant documents or records].

Test: [SELECT FROM: Organizational processes for system monitoring; mechanisms supporting or implementing system monitoring capability].

# CONCLUSION
## This is Risk Management, NOT Risk Elimination

The major premise of the NIST cybersecurity process is to recognize that it's not about the absolute certainty that the security controls will stop every type of cyber-attack. Risk Management is about recognizing the system's overall weaknesses. It's about the C/U 's leadership, not just the IT staff, has identified where those weaknesses exist.

Risk Management is also about a defined Continuous Monitoring (ConMon) and effective Risk Assessment processes. Such processes afford the needed protection to a C/U 's sensitive CUI/CDI. These are not meant to be complete answers to an ever-changing risk landscape. It is only through an active and continual review of the controls can the government or companies ensure near-certainty their networks are as secure *as possible.*

The target of this book is to provide information that they and their IT staffs can critically think about and how to best respond to these 110 designated controls. This book provides a constructive starting point for small through big C/U to not only meet the requirements of NIST 800-171, but to truly protect its computers, systems, and data from the "bad guys" near and far.

Finally, the expectation is that while DOD may have been the first federal agency to mandate NIST 800-171 implementation; however, expect other agencies such as the Department of Homeland Security (DHS), the Department of Commerce (DOC), home of NIST, and Department of Energy (DOE), to be the next likely candidates to necessitate C/U to meet NIST 800-171. The rest of the federal agencies will most likely follow closely behind. NIST 800-171 is becoming the national cybersecurity standard between federal government operations and its huge contractor support workforce in the very near future.

## *Be a Good Boy Scout, Always Be Prepared*

# APPENDIX A – Relevant References

---

Federal Information Security Modernization Act of 2014 (P.L. 113-283), December 2014.
http://www.gpo.gov/fdsys/pkg/PLAW-113publ283/pdf/PLAW-113publ283.pdf

Executive Order 13556, *Controlled Unclassified Information*, November 2010.
http://www.gpo.gov/fdsys/pkg/FR-2010-11-09/pdf/2010-28360.pdf

Executive Order 13636, *Improving Critical Infrastructure Cybersecurity*, February 2013.
http://www.gpo.gov/fdsys/pkg/FR-2013-02-19/pdf/2013-03915.pdf

National Institute of Standards and Technology Federal Information Processing Standards Publication 200 (as amended), *Minimum Security Requirements for Federal Information and Information Systems*.
http://csrc.nist.gov/publications/fips/fips200/FIPS-200-final-march.pdf

National Institute of Standards and Technology Special Publication 800-53 (as amended), *Security and Privacy Controls for Federal Information Systems and Organizations*.
http://dx.doi.org/10.6028/NIST.SP.800-53r4

National Institute of Standards and Technology Special Publication 800-171, rev. 1, *Protecting Controlled Unclassified Information in Nonfederal Information Systems and Organizations*.
https://nvlpubs.nist.gov/nistpubs/SpecialPublications/NIST.SP.800-171r1.pdf

National Institute of Standards and Technology Special Publication 800-171A, *Assessing Security Requirements for Controlled Unclassified Information*
https://csrc.nist.gov/CSRC/media/Publications/sp/800-171a/draft/sp800-171A-draft.pdf

National Institute of Standards and Technology *Framework for Improving Critical Infrastructure Cybersecurity* (as amended).
http://www.nist.gov/cyberframework

**Audit log.**   A chronological record of information system activities, including records of system accesses and operations performed in a given period.

**Authentication.**   Verifying the identity of a user, process, or device, often as a prerequisite to allowing access to resources in an information system.

**Availability.**   Ensuring timely and reliable access to and use of information.

**Baseline Configuration.**   A documented set of specifications for an information system, or a configuration item within a system, that has been formally reviewed and agreed on at a given point in time, and which can be changed only through change control procedures.

**Blacklisting.**   The process used to identify: (i) software programs that are not authorized to execute on an information system; or (ii) prohibited websites.

**Confidentiality.**   Preserving authorized restrictions on information access and disclosure, including means for protecting personal privacy and proprietary information.

**Configuration Management.**   A collection of activities focused on establishing and maintaining the integrity of information technology products and information systems, through control of processes for initializing, changing, and monitoring the configurations of those products and systems throughout the system development life cycle.

**Controlled Unclassified Information (CUI/CDI).**

Information that law, regulation, or governmentwide policy requires to have safeguarding or disseminating controls, excluding information that is classified under Executive Order 13526, Classified National Security Information, December 29, 2009, or any predecessor or successor order, or the Atomic Energy Act of 1954, as amended.

**External network.**   A network not controlled by the C/U .

**FIPS-validated cryptography.**   A cryptographic module validated by the Cryptographic Module Validation Program (CMVP) to meet requirements specified in FIPS Publication 140-2 (as amended). As a prerequisite to CMVP validation, the cryptographic module is required to employ a cryptographic algorithm implementation that has successfully passed validation testing by the Cryptographic Algorithm Validation Program (CAVP).

**Hardware.**
The physical components of an information system.

**Incident.**
An occurrence that actually or potentially jeopardizes the confidentiality, integrity, or availability of an information system or the information the system processes, stores, or transmits or that constitutes a violation or imminent threat of violation of security policies, security procedures, or acceptable use policies.

**Information Security.**
The protection of information and information systems from unauthorized access, use, disclosure, disruption, modification, or destruction to provide confidentiality, integrity, and availability.

**Information System.**
A discrete set of information resources organized for the collection, processing, maintenance, use, sharing, dissemination, or disposition of information.

**Information Technology.**
Any equipment or interconnected system or subsystem of equipment that is used in the automatic acquisition, storage, manipulation, management, movement, control, display, switching, interchange, transmission, or reception of data or information by the executive agency. It includes computers, ancillary equipment, software, firmware, and similar procedures, services (including support services), and related resources.

**Integrity.**
Guarding against improper information modification or destruction and includes ensuring information non-repudiation and authenticity.

**Internal Network.**
A network where: (i) the establishment, maintenance, and provisioning of security controls are under the direct control of organizational employees or contractors; or (ii) cryptographic encapsulation or similar security technology implemented between organization-controlled endpoints, provides the same effect (at least about confidentiality and integrity).

**Malicious Code.**
Software intended to perform an unauthorized process that will have adverse impact on the confidentiality, integrity, or availability of an information system. A virus, worm, Trojan horse, or other code-based entity that infects a host. Spyware and some forms of adware are also examples of malicious code.

**Media.**
Physical devices or writing surfaces including, but not limited to, magnetic tapes, optical disks, magnetic disks, and printouts (but not including display media) onto which information is recorded, stored, or printed within an information system.

**Mobile Code.**                    Software programs or parts of programs obtained from remote information systems, transmitted across a network, and executed on a local information system without explicit installation or execution by the recipient.

**Mobile device.**                   A portable computing device that: (i) has a small form factor such that it can easily be carried by a single individual; (ii) is designed to operate without a physical connection (e.g., wirelessly transmit or receive information); (iii) possesses local, nonremovable or removable data storage; and (iv) includes a self-contained power source. Mobile devices may also include voice communication capabilities, on-board sensors that allow the devices to capture information, and/or built-in features for synchronizing local data with remote locations. Examples include smartphones, tablets, and E-readers.

**Multifactor Authentication.**    Authentication using two or more different factors to achieve authentication. Factors include: (i) something you know (e.g., password/PIN); (ii) something you have (e.g., cryptographic identification device, token); or (iii) something you are (e.g., biometric).

**Nonfederal Information System.**  An information system that does not meet the criteria for a federal information system. nonfederal organization.

**Network.**                       Information system(s) implemented with a collection of interconnected components. Such components may include routers, hubs, cabling, telecommunications controllers, key distribution centers, and technical control devices.

**Portable storage device.**    An information system component that can be inserted into and removed from an information system, and that is used to store data or information (e.g., text, video, audio, and/or image data). Such components are typically implemented on magnetic, optical, or solid-state devices (e.g., floppy disks, compact/digital video disks, flash/thumb drives, external hard disk drives, and flash memory cards/drives that contain nonvolatile memory).

**Privileged Account.**           An information system account with authorizations of a privileged user.

**Privileged User.**              A user that is authorized (and therefore, trusted) to perform security-relevant functions that ordinary users are not authorized to perform.

**Remote Access.**                Access to an organizational information system by a user (or a process acting on behalf of a user) communicating through an external network (e.g., the Internet).

**Risk.**
A measure of the extent to which an entity is threatened by a potential circumstance or event, and typically a function of: (i) the adverse impacts that would arise if the circumstance or event occurs; and (ii) the likelihood of occurrence. Information system-related security risks are those risks that arise from the loss of confidentiality, integrity, or availability of information or information systems and reflect the potential adverse impacts to organizational operations (including mission, functions, image, or reputation), organizational assets, individuals, other organizations, and the Nation.

**Sanitization.**
Actions taken to render data written on media unrecoverable by both ordinary and, for some forms of sanitization, extraordinary means. Process to remove information from media such that data recovery is not possible. It includes removing all classified labels, markings, and activity logs.

**Security Control.**
A safeguard or countermeasure prescribed for an information system or an organization designed to protect the confidentiality, integrity, and availability of its information and to meet a set of defined security requirements.

**Security Control Assessment.**
The testing or evaluation of security controls to determine the extent to which the controls are implemented correctly, operating as intended, and producing the desired outcome with respect to meeting the security requirements for an information system or organization.

**Security Functions.**
The hardware, software, and/or firmware of the information system responsible for enforcing the system security policy and supporting the isolation of code and data on which the protection is based.

**Threat.**
Any circumstance or event with the potential to adversely impact organizational operations (including mission, functions, image, or reputation), organizational assets, individuals, other organizations, or the Nation through an information system via unauthorized access, destruction, disclosure, modification of information, and/or denial of service.

**Whitelisting.**
The process used to identify: (i) software programs that are authorized to execute on an information system.

# Intelligence Cycle Approach for the POAM Lifecycle

This section is designed to suggest a structure and approach for anyone developing a POAM for their C/U or agency. It describes how to address the POAM development process and how to formulate and track POAMs during their lifecycle. We suggest using the US Intelligence Community's *Intelligence Lifecycle* as a guide to address POAM's from "cradle-to-grave." The process has been slightly modified to provide a more pertinent description for the purposes of POAM creation, but we have found this model to be effective for the novice through professional cybersecurity or IT specialist that works regularly in this arena.

This includes the following six stages:

1.  **IDENTIFY:** Those controls that time, technology or cost cannot be met to satisfy the unimplemented control.

2.  **RESEARCH:** You now have decided the control is not going to meet your immediate NIST 800-171 needs. The typical initial milestone is to conduct some form of research or market survey of available solutions. This will include:

    -   **The kind or type of solution.** Either as a person (e.g., additional expertise), process (e.g., what established workflow can provide a repeatable solution) or technology (e.g. what hardware/software solution fixes all or part of the control.

    -   **How the federal government wants it implemented**? For example, are hard tokens required or can the C/U use some form of soft token solution to address 2FA.

    -   **Internal challenges.** What does the C/U face overall with people, process, or technology perspectives specific to the control?

3.  **RECOMMEND:** At this phase, all research and analysis has been completed, and presumably well-documented. Typically, the cybersecurity team or C/U IT team will formulate recommended solutions to the System Owner, i.e., the C/U decision-makers such as the Chief Information or Operations Officer. The recommendations must not only be technically feasible, but cost and resources should be part of any recommendation.

4.  **DECIDE:** At this point, C/U decision-makers not only approve of the approach to correct the security shortfall but have agreed to resourcing requirements to authorize the expenditures of funds and efforts.

5.  **IMPLEMENT:** Finally, the solution is implemented, and the POAM is updated for closure. This should be reported to the Contract Office or its representative on a recurring basis.

6. **CONTINUAL IMPROVEMENT.** Like any process, it should be regularly reviewed and updated specific to the needs and capabilities of the C/U or organization. This could include better templates, additional staffing, or more regular updates to management to ensure both a thorough but supportive understanding of how cybersecurity meets the needs and mission of the C/U.

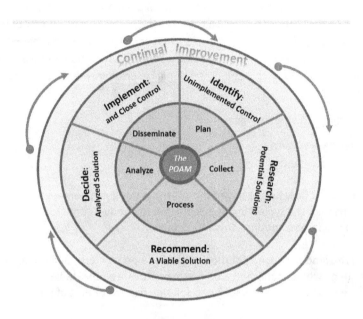

**The POAM Lifecycle**

We begin in the "Identify" section of the lifecycle process above. At this stage several things may occur. Either the C/U system owner or IT staff recognizes that the security control is not or cannot be immediately met, or they employ an automated security tool, such as ACAS® or Nessus®, that identifies securities vulnerabilities within the information system. This could also include findings such as the default password, like "password," has not been changed on an internal switch or router. It could also include updated security patching has not occurred; some automated application scanning tools will not only identify but recommend courses of action to mitigate or fix a security finding. Always try to leverage those as soon as possible to secure the IT environment.

Also, assumed in this stage is the act of documenting findings. The finding should be placed in a POAM template as the C/U move through the lifecycle. This could be done using documents created in Word®, for example, but we recommend using a spreadsheet program that allows for the easier filtering and management of the POAM. Spreadsheets afford greater flexibility during the "heavy lift" portion of formulating all POAM's not intended to be fixed immediately because of technical shortfalls. This may include not having in-house technical expertise, for example, to setup Two Factor Authentication (2FA) or because of current C/U financial limitations; this would most likely be reasonable when the costs are currently prohibitive to implement a specific control.

In the "research" phase this includes technical analysis, Internet searches, market research, etc., regarding viable solutions to address the security control not being "compliant." This activity is typically part of initial milestone established in the POAM. It may be added in the POAM, and could be, for example: "Conduct an initial market research of candidate systems that can provide an affordable Two Factor Authentication (2FA) solution to meet security control 3.X.X." Another example might be: "The cybersecurity section will identify at least two candidate Data at Rest (DAR) solutions to protect the C/U 's CUI data." These initial milestones are a normal part of any initial milestones that clearly describes reasonable actions to address non-complaint controls.

Another part of any milestone establishment action is to identify when a milestone is expected to be complete. Typically, milestones are done for a 30-day period, but if the complexity of such an activity requires additional time, ensure the C/U has identified reasonable periods of times with actual dates of *expected* completion. Never use undefined milestones such as "next version update" or "Calendar Year 2020 in Quarter 4." Real dates are mandatory to truly manage findings supported by, for example, automated workflow or tracking applications the C/U may acquire in the future to enhance its cybersecurity risk management program.

At the "recommendation" phase, this is the time when the prior research has resulted in at least one solution, be it additional skilled personnel (people), enhanced C/U policies that manage the security control better (process), or a device that solves the control in part or total (technology). This should be part of this phase and be part of the POAM template as a milestone with the expected completion date.

At the "decide" phase, C/U or agency decision-makers should approve a recommended solution and that decision should be documented in a configuration change tracking document, configuration management decision memorandum or in the POAM itself. This should include approved resources, but most importantly, any funding decision should be acted upon as quickly as possible. While many of these suggestions may seem basic, it is often overlooked to document the decision so future personnel and management can understand how the solution was determined.

The "implementation" phase may become the most difficult. It is where a lead should be designated to coordinate the specific activity to meet the control— it may not necessarily be a technical solution, but may also include, for example, a documentation development activity that creates a process to manage the POAM.

Implementation should also include basic programmatic considerations. This should include performance, schedule, cost, and risk:

- Performance: consider what success the solution is attempting to address. Will it can send email alerts to users? Will the system shutdown automatically once an intrusion is confirmed in the C/U network? Will the Incident Response Plan include notifications to law enforcement? Performance is always a significant and measurable means to ensure that the solution will address the POAM/security control shortfall. Always try to measure performance specific to the actual control that is being met.

- Schedule: Devise a plan based upon the developed milestones that are reasonable and not unrealistic. As soon as a deviation becomes apparent, ensure that the POAM template is updated and approved by management. This should be a senior management representative with the authority to provide extensions to the current plan.  This could include, for example, a Senior IT Manager, Chief Information Security Officer, or Chief Operating Officer.

- Cost: While it is assumed all funding has been provided early in the process, always ensure contingencies are in place to request additional funding.  It is common in most IT programs to maintain a 15-20% funding reserve for emergencies.  Otherwise, the Project Manager or lead will have to re-justify to management for additional funding late in the implementation portion of the cycle.

- Risk: This is not the risk identified, for example, by the review of security controls or automated scans of the system.  This risk is specific to the program's success to accomplish its goal to close the security finding.  Risk should always in particular focus on the performance, cost, and schedule risks as major concerns. Consider creating a risk matrix or risk log to help during the implementation phase.

Finally, ensure that as soon as the C/U can satisfactorily implement its solution close the control and notify the Contract Office of the completion.  Typically, updates and notifications should occur at least once a quarter, but more often is appropriate for more highly impactful controls.  Two-factor authentication and automated auditing, for example, are best updated as quickly as possible.  This not only secures the C/U 's network and IT environment but builds confidence with the government that security requirements are being met.

A final area to consider in terms of best-practices within cybersecurity, and more specifically in developing complete POAMs, is the area of **continual improvement**.  Leveraging the legacy Intelligence Lifecycle process should be an ongoing model for IT and cybersecurity specialists to emulate. Those supporting this process should always be prepared to make changes or modifications that better represent the state and readiness of the system with its listing of POAMs. The Intelligence Lifecycle provides the ideal model for a C/U to follow and implement to meet its POAM responsibilities within NIST 800-171.

---

## For the Technically-Capable College/University (C/U):

**Consider importing POAM spreadsheets into a database program and using its internal reporting creation and report capabilities.  It can be used to enhance POAM status reporting and tracking for Senior Management.**

# Continuous Monitoring (ConMon): A More Detailed Discussion

Cybersecurity is not about shortcuts. There are no easy solutions to years of leaders demurring their responsibility to address the growing threats in cyberspace. We hoped that the Office of Personnel Management (OPM) breach several years ago would herald the needed focus, energy, and funding to quash the bad-guys. That has proven an empty hope where leaders have abrogated their responsibility to lead in cyberspace. The "holy grail" solution of Continuous Monitoring (ConMon) has been the most misunderstood solution where too many shortcuts are perpetrated by numerous federal agencies and the private sector to create an illusion of success. This paper is specifically written to help leaders better understand what constitutes a true statement of: "we have continuous monitoring." This is not about shortcuts. This is about education, training, and understanding at the highest leadership levels that cybersecurity is not a technical issue, but a leadership issue.

The Committee on National Security Systems defines ConMon as: "[t]he processes implemented to maintain current security status for one or more information systems on which the operational mission of the enterprise depends," (CNSS, 2010). ConMon has been described as the holistic solution of end-to-end cybersecurity coverage and the answer to providing an effective global Risk Management (RM) solution. It promises the elimination of the 3-year recertification cycle that has been the bane of cybersecurity professionals.

For ConMon to become a reality for any agency, it must meet the measures and expectations as defined in National Institute of Standards and Technology (NIST) Special Publication (SP) 800-137, Information Security Continuous Monitoring for Federal Information Systems and Organizations. "Continuous monitoring has evolved as a best practice for managing risk on an ongoing basis," (SANS Institute, 2016); it is an instrument that supports effective, continual, and recurring RM assurances. For any agency to truly espouse it has attained full ConMon compliance, it must be able to coordinate all the described major elements as found in NIST SP 800-137.

ConMon is not just the passive visibility pieces, but also includes the active efforts of vulnerability scanning, threat alert, reduction, mitigation, or elimination of a dynamic Information Technology (IT) environment. The Department of Homeland Security (DHS) has couched its approach to ConMon more holistically. Their program to protect government networks is more aptly called: "Continuous Diagnostics and Monitoring" or CDM and includes a need to react to an active network attacker. "The ability to make IT networks, end-points and applications visible; to identify malicious activity; and, to respond [emphasis added] immediately is critical to defending information systems and networks," (Sann, 2016).

Another description of ConMon can be found in NIST's CAESARS Framework Extension: An Enterprise Continuous Monitoring Technical Reference Model (Second Draft). It defines its essential characteristics within the concept of "Continuous Security Monitoring." It is described as a "...risk management approach to Cybersecurity that maintains a picture of an organization's security posture, provides visibility into assets, leverages use of automated data feeds, monitors effectiveness of security controls, and enables prioritization of remedies," (NIST, 2012); it must demonstrate visibility, data feeds, measures of effectiveness and allow for solutions. It provides another description of what should be demonstrated to ensure full ConMon designation under the NIST standard.

The government's Federal Risk and Authorization Management Program (Fed-RAMP) has defined similar ConMon goals. These objectives are all key outcomes of a successful ConMon implementation. Its "... goal[s]...[are] to provide: (i) operational visibility; (ii) annual self-attestations on security control implementations; (iii) managed change control; (iv) and attendance to incident response duties," (GSA, 2012). These objectives, while not explicit to NIST SP 800-37, are well-aligned with the desires of an effective and complete solution.

RMF creates the structure and documentation needs of ConMon; it represents the specific implementation and oversight of Information Security (IS) within an IT environment. It supports the general activity of RM within an agency. (See Figure 1 below). The RMF "... describes a disciplined and structured process that integrates information security and risk management activities into the system development life cycle," (NIST-B, 2011). RMF is the structure that both describes and relies upon ConMon as its risk oversight and effectiveness mechanism between IS and RM.

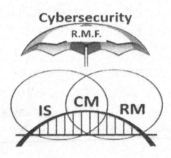

**Figure 1. CM "bridges" Information Security and Risk Management**

This article provides a conceptual framework to address how an agency would approach identifying a true ConMon solution through NIST SP 800-137. It discusses the additional need to align component requirements with the *"11 Security Automation Domains"* that are necessary to implement true ConMon. (See Figure 2 below). It is through the complete implementation and

**Figure 2. The 11 Security Automation Domains (NIST, 2011)**

integration with the other described components—See Figure 3 below--that an organization can correctly state it has achieved ConMon.

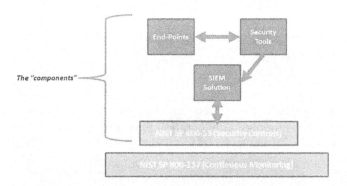

**Figure 3. The "Components" of an Effective Continuous Monitoring**

## Continuous Monitoring – First Generation

For ConMon to be effective and genuine, it must align end-point visibility with security monitoring tools. This includes security monitoring tools with connectivity to "end-points" such as laptops, desktops, servers, routers, firewalls, etc. Additionally, these must work with a highly integrated Security Information and Event Management (SIEM) device. The other "component" is a clear linkage between the end-points, security monitoring tools, and the SIEM appliance, working with the *Security Automation Domains* (See Figure 2). These would include, for example, the areas of malware detection, asset and event management.  ConMon must first address these collective components to create a "First Generation" instantiation.

More specifically, a SIEM appliance provides the central core data processing capabilities to effectively coordinate all the inputs and outputs from across the IT enterprise.  It manages the data integration and interpretation of all ConMon components.  And, it provides the necessary visibility and intelligence for an active incident response capability.

***End-point devices must be persistently visible to the applicable security devices.*** Together, these parts must align with the respective security controls as described in NIST SP 800-53.  The selected SIEM tool must be able to accept these inputs and analyze them against defined security policy settings, recurring vulnerability scans, signature-based threats, and heuristic/activity-based analyses to ensure the environment's security posture.  The outputs of the SIEM must support the further visibility of the IT environment, conduct and disseminate vital intelligence, and alert leadership to any ongoing or imminent dangers.  The expression above is designed to provide a conceptual representation of the cybersecurity professional attempting to ascertain effective ConMon implementation or to develop a complete ConMon answer for an agency or C/U.

Additionally, the SIEM must distribute data feeds in near-real time to analysts and key leaders.  It provides for multi-level "dashboard" data streams and issues alert based upon prescribed policy settings.  Once these base, First Generation functionalities are consistently aligning with the Security Automation Domains, then an organization or C/U  can definitively express it meets the requirements of ConMon.

## End-Points

It is necessary to identify hardware and software configuration items that must be known and constantly traceable before implementing ConMon within an enterprise IT environment.  End-point visibility is not the hardware devices, but the baseline software of each hardware device on the network.

Configuration Management is also a foundational requirement for any organization's security posture.  Soundly implemented Configuration Management must be the basis of any complete CM implementation.  At the beginning of any IS effort, cyber-professionals must know the current "as-is" hardware and software component state within the enterprise.  End-points must be protected and monitored because they are the most valuable target for would-be hackers and cyber-thieves.

Configuration Management provides the baseline that establishes a means to identify potential compromise between the enterprise's end-points and the requisite security tools.  "Organizations with a robust and effective [Configuration Management] process need to consider information security implications concerning the development and operation of information systems including hardware, software, applications, and documentation," (NIST-A, 2011).

The RMF requires the categorization of systems and data as high, moderate, or low regarding risk.  The Federal Information Processing Standards (FIPS) Publication 199 methodology is typically used to establish data sensitivity levels in the federal government.  FIPS 199 aids the cybersecurity professional in determining data protection standards of both end-points and the data stored in these respective parts. For example, a system that collects and retains sensitive data, such as financial information, requires a greater level of security. It is important that end-points are recognized as repositories of highly valued data to cyber-threats.

Further, cyber-security professionals must be constantly aware of the "...administrative and technological costs of offering a high degree of protection for all federal systems...," (Ross, Katzke, & Toth, 2005). This is not a matter of recognizing the physical end-point alone but the value and associated costs of the virtual data stored, monitored, and protected on a continual basis. FIPS 199 assists system owners in determining whether a higher level of protection is warranted, with higher associated costs, based upon an overall FIPS 199 evaluation.

## Security Tools

Security monitoring tools must identify in near-real time an active threat. Examples include anti-virus or anti-malware applications used to monitor network and end-point activities. Products like McAfee and Symantec provide enterprise capabilities that help to identify and reduce threats.

Other security tools would address in whole or part the remaining NIST Security Automation Domains. These would include, for example, tools to provide asset visibility, vulnerability detection, patch management updates, etc. But it is also critical to recognize that even the best current security tools are not necessarily capable of defending against all attacks. New malware or zero-day attacks pose continual challenges to the cybersecurity workforce.

For example, DHS's EINSTEIN system would not have stopped the 2015 Office of Personnel Management breach. Even DHS's latest iteration of EINSTEIN, EINSTEIN 3, an advanced network monitoring and response system designed to protect federal governments' networks, would not have stopped that attack. "...EINSTEIN 3 would not have been able to catch a threat that [had] no known footprints, according to multiple industry experts," (Sternstein, 2015).

Not until there are a much greater integration and availability of cross-cutting intelligence and more capable security tools, can any single security tool ever be fully effective. The need for multiple security monitoring tools that provide "defense in depth" may be a better protective strategy. However, with multiple tools monitoring the same Security Automation Domains, such an approach will certainly increase the costs of maintaining a secure agency or C/U IT environment. A determination of Return on Investment (ROI) balanced against a well-defined threat risk scoring approach is further needed at all levels of the federal and C/U IT workspace.

## Security Controls

"Organizations are required to adequately mitigate the risk arising from the use of information and information systems in the execution of missions and C/U functions," (NIST, 2013). This is accomplished by the selection and implementation of NIST SP 800-53, Revision 4, described security controls. (See Figure 4 below). They are organized into eighteen families to address sub-set security areas such as access control, physical security, incident response, etc. The use of these controls is typically tailored to the security categorization by the respective system owner relying upon FIPS 199 categorization standards. A higher security categorization requires the greater implementation of these controls.

| ID | FAMILY | ID | FAMILY |
|---|---|---|---|
| AC | Access Control | MP | Media Protection |
| AT | Awareness and Training | PE | Physical and Environmental Protection |
| AU | Audit and Accountability | PL | Planning |
| CA | Security Assessment and Authorization | PS | Personnel Security |
| CM | Configuration Management | RA | Risk Assessment |
| CP | Contingency Planning | SA | System and Services Acquisition |
| IA | Identification and Authentication | SC | System and Communications Protection |
| IR | Incident Response | SI | System and Information Integrity |
| MA | Maintenance | PM | Program Management |

**Note that these are all the control families required within DOD. Under the NIST 800-171 effort, not all control families are used or required.

Figure 4. Security Control Identifiers and Family Names, (NIST, 2013)

## Security Information and Event Management (SIEM) Solutions

The SIEM tool plays a pivotal role in any viable "First Generation" implementation. Based on NIST and DHS guidance, an effective SIEM appliance must provide the following functionalities:

- "Aggregate data from "across a diverse set" of security tool sources;
- Analyze the multi-source data;
- Engage in explorations of data based on changing needs
- Make quantitative use of data for security (not just reporting) purposes including the development and use of risk scores; and
- Maintain actionable awareness of the changing security situation on a real-time basis," (Levinson, 2011).

"Effectiveness is further enhanced when the output is formatted to provide information that is specific, measurable, actionable, relevant, and timely," (NIST, 2011). The SIEM device is the vital core of a full solution that collects, analyzes, and alerts the cyber-professional of potential and actual dangers in their environment.

There are several major SIEM solutions that can effectively meet the requirements of NIST SP 800-137. They include products, for example, IBM® Security, Splunk®, and Hewlett Packard's® ArcSight® products.

For example, Logrhythm ® was highly rated in the 2014 SIEM evaluation. Logrhythm® provided network event monitoring and alerts of potential security compromises. The implementation of an enterprise-grade SIEM solution is necessary to meet growing cybersecurity requirements for auditing of security logs and capabilities to respond to cyber-incidents. SIEM products will continue to play a critical and evolving role in the demands for "…increased security and rapid response to events throughout the network," (McAfee® Foundstone Professional Services®, 2013). Improvements and upgrades of SIEM tools are critical to providing a more highly responsive capability for future generations of these appliances in the marketplace.

## Next Generations

Future generations of ConMon would include specific expanded capabilities and functionalities of the SIEM device. These second generation and beyond evolutions would be more effective solutions in future dynamic and hostile network environments. Such advancements might also include increased access to a greater pool of threat database signature repositories or more expansive heuristics that could identify active anomalies within a target network.

Another futuristic capability might include the use of Artificial Intelligence (AI). Improved capabilities of a SIEM appliance with AI augmentation would further enhance human threat analysis and provide for more automated responsiveness. "The concept of predictive analysis involves using statistical methods and decision tools that analyze current and historical data to make predictions about future events…," (SANS Institute). The next generation would boost human response times and abilities to defend against attacks in a matter of milli-seconds vice hours.

Finally, in describing the next generations of ConMon, it is not only imperative to expand data, informational and intelligence inputs for new and more capable SIEM products, but that input and corresponding data sets must also be fully vetted for completeness and accuracy. Increased access to signature and heuristic activity-based analysis databases would provide greater risk reduction. Greater support from private industry and the Intelligence Community would also be major improvements for Agencies that are constantly struggling against a more-capable and better-resourced threat.

ConMon will not be a reality until vendors and agencies can integrate the right people, processes, and technologies. "Security needs to be positioned as an enabler of the organization—it must take its place alongside human resources, financial resources, sound C/U processes and strategies, information technology, and intellectual capital as the elements of success for accomplishing the mission," (Caralli, 2004). ConMon is not just a technical solution. It requires capable organizations with trained personnel, creating effective policies and procedures with the requisite technologies to stay ahead of the growing threats in cyberspace.

Figure 6 below provides a graphic depiction of what ConMon components are needed to create a holistic NIST SP 800-137-compliant solution; this demonstrates the First-Generation representation. There are numerous vendors describing that they have the "holy grail" solution, but until they can prove they meet this description in total, it is unlikely they have a complete implementation of a thorough ConMon solution yet.

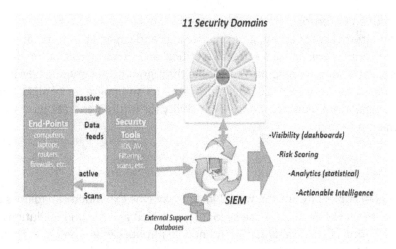

**Figure 6. First Generation Continuous Monitoring**

# Endnotes for "Continuous Monitoring: A More Detailed Discussion"

Balakrishnan, B. (2015, October 6). *Insider Threat Mitigation Guidance* . Retrieved from SANS Institute Infosec Reading Room: https://www.sans.org/reading-room/whitepapers/monitoring/insider-threat-mitigation-guidance-36307

Caralli, R. A. (2004, December). *Managing Enterprise Security (CMU/SEI-2004-TN-046)*. Retrieved from Software Engineering Institute: http://www.sei.cmu.edu/reports/04tn046.pdf

Committee on National Security Systems. (2010, April 26). *National Information Assurance (IA) Glossary*. Retrieved from National Counterintelligence & Security Center: http://www.ncsc.gov/nittf/docs/CNSSI-4009_National_Information_Assurance.pdf

Department of Defense. (2014, March 12). *DOD Instructions 8510.01: Risk Management Framework (RMF) for DoD Information Technology (IT)*. Retrieved from Defense Technical Information Center (DTIC): http://www.dtic.mil/whs/directives/corres/pdf/851001_2014.pdf

GSA. (2012, January 27). *Continuous Monitoring Strategy & Guide, v1.1*. Retrieved from General Services Administration: http://www.gsa.gov/graphics/staffoffices/Continuous_Monitoring_Strategy_Guide_072712.pdf

Joint Medical Logistics Functional Development Center. (2015). JMLFDC Continuous Monitoring Strategy Plan and Procedure. Ft Detrick, MD.

Kavanagh, K. M., Nicolett, M., & Rochford, O. (2014, June 25). *Magic Quadrant for Security Information and Event Management*. Retrieved from Gartner: http://www.gartner.com/technology/reprints.do?id=1-1W8AO4W&ct=140627&st=sb&mkt_tok=3RkMMJWWfF9wsRolsqrJcO%2FhmjTEU5z17u8lWa%2B0gYkz2EFye%2BLIHETpodcMTcVkNb%2FYDBceEJhqyQJxPr3FKdANz8JpRhnqAA%3D%3D

Kolenko, M. M. (2016, February 18). *SPECIAL-The Human Element of Cybersecurity*. Retrieved from Homeland Security Today.US: http://www.hstoday.us/briefings/industry-news/single-article/special-the-human-element-of-cybersecurity/54008efd46e93863f54db0f7352dde2c.html

Levinson, B. (2011, October). *Federal Cybersecurity Best Practices Study: Information Security Continuous Monitoring*. Retrieved from Center for Regulatory Effectiveness: http://www.thecre.com/fisma/wp-content/uploads/2011/10/Federal-Cybersecurity-Best-Practice.ISCM_2.pdf

McAfee® Foundstone® Professional Services. (2013). *McAfee*. Retrieved from White Paper: Creating and Maintaining a SOC: http://www.mcafee.com/us/resources/white-papers/foundstone/wp-creating-maintaining-soc.pdf

NIST. (2011-A, August). *NIST SP 800-128: Guide for Security-Focused Configuration Management of Information Systems.* Retrieved from NIST Computer Security Resource Center: http://csrc.nist.gov/publications/nistpubs/800-128/sp800-128.pdf

NIST. (2011-B, September). *Special Publication 800-137: Information Security Continuous Monitoring (ISCM) for Federal Information Systems and Organizations.* Retrieved from NIST Computer Security Resource Center: http://csrc.nist.gov/publications/nistpubs/800-137/SP800-137-Final.pdf

NIST. (2012, January). *NIST Interagency Report 7756: CAESARS Framework Extension: An Enterprise Continuous Monitoring Technical Reference Model (Second Draft), .* Retrieved from NIST Computer Resource Security Center: http://csrc.nist.gov/publications/drafts/nistir-7756/Draft-NISTIR-7756_second-public-draft.pdf

NIST. (2013, April). *NIST SP 800-53, Rev 4: Security and Privacy Controls for Federal Information Systems .* Retrieved from NIST: http://nvlpubs.nist.gov/nistpubs/SpecialPublications/NIST.SP.800-53r4.pdf

Ross, R., Katzke, S., & Toth, P. (2005, October 17). *The New FISMA Standards and Guidelines Changing the Dynamic of Information Security for the Federal Government.* Retrieved from Information Technology Promotion Agency of Japan: https://www.ipa.go.jp/files/000015362.pdf

Sann, W. (2016, January 8). *The Key Missing Piece of Your Cyber Strategy? Visibility.* Retrieved from Nextgov: http://www.nextgov.com/technology-news/tech-insider/2016/01/key-missing-element-your-cyber-strategy-visibility/124974/

SANS Institute. (2016, March 6). *Beyond Continuous Monitoring: Threat Modeling for Real-time Response.* Retrieved from SANS Institute: http://www.sans.org/reading-room/whitepapers/analyst/continuous-monitoring-threat-modeling-real-time-response-35185

Sternstein, A. (2015, January 6). *OPM Hackers Skirted Cutting-Edge Intrusion Detection System, Official Says .* Retrieved from Nextgov: http://www.nextgov.com/cybersecurity/2015/06/opm-hackers-skirted-cutting-edge-interior-intrusion-detection-official-says/114649/

# APPENDIX E – NIST 800-171 Compliance Checklist

The following compliance checklist is intended to provide a guide to conduct a "self-assessment" of the C/U 's overall cybersecurity posture as required by NIST 800-171.

*Assessment Method: Refer to NIST 800-171A, *Assessing Security Requirements for Controlled Unclassified Information*, that describes types and means to self-validate the control. The three assessment methods are: examine, interview and test.

| Control # | Description | Assessment Method* | Document (e.g., SSP or Co. Procedure Guide) | Page # | Reviewed By | Validated By |
|---|---|---|---|---|---|---|
| **Access Control (AC)** | | | | | | |
| 3.1.1 | *Limit information system access to authorized users, processes acting on behalf of authorized users, or devices (including other information systems)* | | | | | |
| 3.1.1[a] | *Authorized users are identified.* | | | | | |
| 3.1.1[b] | *Processes acting on behalf of authorized users are identified.* | | | | | |
| 3.1.1[c] | *Devices (and other systems) authorized to connect to the system are identified.* | | | | | |
| 3.1.1[d] | *System access is limited to authorized users.* | | | | | |
| 3.1.1[e] | *System access is limited to processes acting on behalf of authorized users.* | | | | | |
| 3.1.1[f] | *System access is limited to authorized devices (including other systems).* | | | | | |
| 3.1.1[a] | *Authorized users are identified.* | | | | | |
| 3.1.2 | *Limit information system access to the types of transactions and functions that authorized users are permitted to execute* | | | | | |
| 3.1.2[a] | *The types of transactions and functions that authorized users are permitted to execute are defined.* | | | | | |
| 3.1.2[b] | *System access is limited to the defined types of transactions and functions for authorized users.* | | | | | |

| 3.1.3 | *Control the flow of CUI in accordance with approved authorizations* | |
|---|---|---|
| 3.1.3[a] | *Information flow control policies are defined.* | |
| 3.1.3[b] | *Methods and enforcement mechanisms for controlling the flow of CUI are defined.* | |
| 3.1.3[c] | *Designated sources and destinations (e.g., networks, individuals, and devices) for CUI within the system and between interconnected systems are identified.* | |
| 3.1.3[d] | *Authorizations for controlling the flow of CUI are defined.* | |
| 3.1.3[e] | *Approved authorizations for controlling the flow of CUI are enforced.* | |
| **3.1.4** | **Separate the duties of individuals to reduce the risk of malevolent activity without collusion** | |
| 3.1.4[a] | *The duties of individuals requiring separation are defined.* | |
| 3.1.4[b] | *Responsibilities for duties that require separation are assigned to separate individuals.* | |
| 3.1.4[c] | *Access privileges that enable individuals to exercise the duties that require separation are granted to separate individuals.* | |
| **3.1.5** | ***Employ the principle of least privilege, including for specific security functions and privileged accounts*** | |
| 3.1.5[a] | *Privileged accounts are identified.* | |
| 3.1.5[b] | *Access to privileged accounts is authorized in accordance with the principle of least privilege.* | |
| 3.1.5[c] | *Security functions are identified.* | |
| 3.1.5[d] | *Access to security functions is authorized in accordance with the principle of least privilege.* | |
| **3.1.6** | ***Use non-privileged accounts or roles when accessing nonsecurity functions*** | |
| 3.1.6[a] | *Nonsecurity functions are identified.* | |
| 3.1.6[b] | *Users are required to use non-privileged accounts or roles when accessing nonsecurity functions.* | |

| 3.1.7 | Prevent non-privileged users from executing privileged functions and audit the execution of such functions | |
|---|---|---|
| 3.1.7[a] | Privileged functions are defined. | |
| 3.1.7[b] | Non-privileged users are defined. | |
| 3.1.7[c] | Non-privileged users are prevented from executing privileged functions. | |
| 3.1.7[d] | The execution of privileged functions is captured in audit logs. | |
| 3.1.8 | Limit unsuccessful logon attempts | |
| 3.1.8[a] | The means of limiting unsuccessful logon attempts is defined. | |
| 3.1.8[b] | The defined means of limiting unsuccessful logon attempts is implemented. | |
| 3.1.9 | Provide privacy and security notices consistent with applicable CUI rules | |
| 3.1.9[a] | Privacy and security notices required by CUI-specified rules are identified, consistent, and associated with the specific CUI category. | |
| 3.1.9[b] | Privacy and security notices are displayed. | |
| 3.1.10 | Use session lock with pattern-hiding displays to prevent access/viewing of data after period of inactivity | |
| 3.1.10[a] | The period of inactivity after which the system initiates a session lock is defined. | |
| 3.1.10[b] | Access to the system and viewing of data is prevented by initiating a session lock after the defined period of inactivity. | |
| 3.1.10[c] | Previously visible information is concealed via a pattern-hiding display after the defined period of inactivity. | |
| 3.1.11 | Terminate (automatically) a user session after a defined condition | |
| 3.1.11[a] | Conditions requiring a user session to terminate are defined. | |
| 3.1.11[b] | A user session is automatically terminated after any of the defined conditions occur. | |

| Control # | Description | Assessment Method* | Document (e.g., SSP or Co. Procedure Guide) | Page # | Reviewed By | Validated By |
|---|---|---|---|---|---|---|
| **Access Control (AC)** | | | | | | |
| **3.1.12** | *Monitor and control remote access sessions* | | | | | |
| **3.1.12[a]** | *Remote access sessions are permitted.* | | | | | |
| **3.1.12[b]** | *The types of permitted remote access are identified.* | | | | | |
| **3.1.12[c]** | *Remote access sessions are controlled.* | | | | | |
| **3.1.12[d]** | *Remote access sessions are monitored.* | | | | | |
| **3.1.13** | *Employ cryptographic mechanisms to protect the confidentiality of remote access sessions* | | | | | |
| **3.1.13[a]** | *Cryptographic mechanisms to protect the confidentiality of remote access sessions are identified.* | | | | | |
| **3.1.13[b]** | *Cryptographic mechanisms to protect the confidentiality of remote access sessions are implemented.* | | | | | |
| **3.1.14** | *Route remote access via managed access control points* | | | | | |
| **3.1.14[a]** | *Managed access control points are identified and implemented.* | | | | | |
| **3.1.14[b]** | *Remote access is routed through managed network access control points.* | | | | | |
| **3.1.15** | *Authorize remote execution of privileged commands and remote access to security-relevant information* | | | | | |
| **3.1.15[a]** | *Privileged commands authorized for remote execution are identified.* | | | | | |
| **3.1.15[b]** | *Security-relevant information authorized to be accessed remotely is identified.* | | | | | |
| **3.1.15[c]** | *The execution of the identified privileged commands via remote access is authorized.* | | | | | |
| **3.1.15[d]** | *Access to the identified security-relevant information via remote access is authorized.* | | | | | |
| **3.1.16** | *Authorize wireless access prior to allowing such connections* | | | | | |
| **3.1.16[a]** | *Wireless access points are identified.* | | | | | |
| **3.1.16[b]** | *Wireless access is authorized prior to allowing such connections.* | | | | | |

| | | |
|---|---|---|
| **3.1.17** | ***Protect wireless access using authentication and encryption*** | |
| **3.1.17[a]** | *Wireless access to the system is protected using authentication.* | |
| **3.1.17[b]** | *Wireless access to the system is protected using encryption.* | |
| **3.1.18** | ***Control connection of mobile devices*** | |
| **3.1.18[a]** | *Mobile devices that process, store, or transmit CUI are identified.* | |
| **3.1.18[b]** | *Mobile device connections are authorized.* | |
| **3.1.18[c]** | *Mobile device connections are monitored and logged.* | |
| **3.1.19** | ***Encrypt CUI on mobile devices*** | |
| **3.1.19[a]** | *Mobile devices and mobile computing platforms that process, store, or transmit CUI are identified.* | |
| **3.1.19[b]** | *Encryption is employed to protect CUI on identified mobile devices and mobile computing platforms.* | |
| **3.1.20[a]** | *Connections to external systems are identified.* | |
| **3.1.20[b]** | *The use of external systems is identified.* | |
| **3.1.20[c]** | *Connections to external systems are verified.* | |
| **3.1.20[d]** | *The use of external systems is verified.* | |
| **3.1.20[e]** | *Connections to external systems are controlled/limited.* | |
| **3.1.20[f]** | *The use of external systems is controlled/limited.* | |
| **3.1.20[a]** | *Connections to external systems are identified.* | |
| **3.1.21** | ***Limit use of organizational portable storage devices on external systems*** | |
| **3.1.21[a]** | *The use of portable storage devices containing CUI on external systems is identified and documented.* | |
| **3.1.21[b]** | *Limits on the use of portable storage devices containing CUI on external systems are defined.* | |
| **3.1.21[c]** | *The use of portable storage devices containing CUI on external systems is limited as defined.* | |

| 3.1.22 | Control CUI posted or processed on publicly accessible systems | |
|---|---|---|
| 3.1.22[a] | Individuals authorized to post or process information on publicly accessible systems are identified. | |
| 3.1.22[b] | Procedures to ensure CUI is not posted or processed on publicly accessible systems are identified. | |
| 3.1.22[c] | A review process is in place prior to posting of any content to publicly accessible systems. | |
| 3.1.22[d] | Content on publicly accessible systems is reviewed to ensure that it does not include CUI. | |
| 3.1.22[e] | Mechanisms are in place to remove and address improper posting of CUI. | |
| 3.1.22[a] | Individuals authorized to post or process information on publicly accessible systems are identified. | |

| Control # | Description | Assessment Method* | Document (e.g. SSP or Co. Procedure Guide) | Page # | Reviewed By | Validated By |
|---|---|---|---|---|---|---|
| **Awareness & Training (AT)** | | | | | | |
| 3.2.1 | *Ensure that managers, systems administrators, and users of organizational information systems are made aware of the security risks associated with their activities and of the applicable policies, standards, and procedures related to the security of organizational information systems* | | | | | |
| 3.2.1[a] | *Security risks associated with organizational activities involving CUI are identified.* | | | | | |
| 3.2.1[b] | *Policies, standards, and procedures related to the security of the system are identified.* | | | | | |
| 3.2.1[c] | *Managers, systems administrators, and users of the system are made aware of the security risks associated with their activities.* | | | | | |
| 3.2.1[d] | *Managers, systems administrators, and users of the system are made aware of the applicable policies, standards, and procedures related to the security of the system.* | | | | | |
| 3.2.2 | *Ensure that organizational personnel are adequately trained to carry out their assigned information security-related duties and responsibilities* | | | | | |
| 3.2.2[a] | *Information security-related duties, roles, and responsibilities are defined.* | | | | | |
| 3.2.2[b] | *Information security-related duties, roles, and responsibilities are assigned to designated personnel.* | | | | | |
| 3.2.2[c] | *Personnel are adequately trained to carry out their assigned information security-related duties, roles, and responsibilities.* | | | | | |
| 3.2.3 | *Provide security awareness training on recognizing and reporting potential indicators of insider threat* | | | | | |
| 3.2.3[a] | *Potential indicators associated with insider threats are identified.* | | | | | |

| 3.2.3[b] | Security awareness training on recognizing and reporting potential indicators of insider threat is provided to managers and employees. | |
|---|---|---|

| Control # | Description | Assessment Method* | Document (e.g., SSP or Co. Procedure Guide) | Page # | Reviewed By | Validated By |
|---|---|---|---|---|---|---|

## Audit & Accountability (AU)

| | | | | | | |
|---|---|---|---|---|---|---|
| 3.3.1 | *Create, protect, and retain information system audit records to the extent needed to enable the monitoring, analysis, investigation, and reporting of unlawful, unauthorized, or inappropriate information system activity* | | | | | |
| 3.3.1[a] | *Audit logs needed (i.e., event types to be logged) to enable the monitoring, analysis, investigation, and reporting of unlawful or unauthorized system activity are specified.* | | | | | |
| 3.3.1[b] | *The content of audit records needed to support monitoring, analysis, investigation, and reporting of unlawful or unauthorized system activity is defined.* | | | | | |
| 3.3.1[c] | *Audit records are created (generated).* | | | | | |
| 3.3.1[d] | *Audit records, once created, contain the defined content.* | | | | | |
| 3.3.1[e] | *Retention requirements for audit records are defined.* | | | | | |
| 3.3.1[f] | *Audit records are retained as defined.* | | | | | |
| 3.3.2 | *Ensure that the actions of individual information system users can be uniquely traced to those users, so they can be held accountable for their actions* | | | | | |
| 3.3.2[a] | *The content of the audit records needed to support the ability to uniquely trace users to their actions is defined.* | | | | | |
| 3.3.2[b] | *Audit records, once created, contain the defined content.* | | | | | |
| 3.3.3 | *Review and update audited events* | | | | | |
| 3.3.3[a] | *A process for determining when to review logged events is defined.* | | | | | |
| 3.3.3[b] | *Event types being logged are reviewed in accordance with the defined review process.* | | | | | |

| | | |
|---|---|---|
| **3.3.3[c]** | *Event types being logged are updated based on the review.* | |
| **3.3.4** | **Alert in the event of an audit process failure** | |
| **3.3.4[a]** | *Personnel or roles to be alerted in the event of an audit logging process failure are identified.* | |
| **3.3.4[b]** | *Types of audit logging process failures for which alert will be generated are defined.* | |
| **3.3.4[c]** | *Identified personnel or roles are alerted in the event of an audit logging process failure.* | |
| **3.3.5** | **Correlate audit review, analysis, and reporting processes for investigation and response to indications of inappropriate, suspicious, or unusual activity** | |
| **3.3.5[a]** | *Audit record review, analysis, and reporting processes for investigation and response to indications of unlawful, unauthorized, suspicious, or unusual activity are defined.* | |
| **3.3.5[b]** | *Defined audit record review, analysis, and reporting processes are correlated.* | |
| **3.3.6** | **Provide audit reduction and report generation to support on-demand analysis and reporting** | |
| **3.3.6[a]** | *An audit record reduction capability that supports on-demand analysis is provided.* | |
| **3.3.6[b]** | *A report generation capability that supports on-demand reporting is provided.* | |
| **3.3.7** | **Provide an information system capability that compares and synchronizes internal system clocks with an authoritative source to generate time stamps for audit records** | |
| **3.3.7[a]** | *Internal system clocks are used to generate time stamps for audit records.* | |
| **3.3.7[b]** | *An authoritative source with which to compare and synchronize internal system clocks is specified.* | |
| **3.3.7[c]** | *Internal system clocks used to generate time stamps for audit records are* | |

| | | |
|---|---|---|
| | *compared to and synchronized with the specified authoritative time source.* | |
| **3.3.8** | **Protect audit information and audit tools from unauthorized access, modification, and deletion** | |
| **3.3.8[a]** | *Audit information is protected from unauthorized access.* | |
| **3.3.8[b]** | *Audit information is protected from unauthorized modification.* | |
| **3.3.8[c]** | *Audit information is protected from unauthorized deletion.* | |
| **3.3.8[d]** | *Audit logging tools are protected from unauthorized access.* | |
| **3.3.8[e]** | *Audit logging tools are protected from unauthorized modification.* | |
| **3.3.8[f]** | *Audit logging tools are protected from unauthorized deletion.* | |
| **3.3.9** | **Limit management of audit functionality to a subset of privileged users** | |
| **3.3.9[a]** | *A subset of privileged users granted access to manage audit logging functionality is defined.* | |
| **3.3.9[b]** | *Management of audit logging functionality is limited to the defined subset of privileged users.* | |

| Control # | Description | Assessment Method* | Document (e.g., SSP or Co. Procedure Guide) | Page # | Reviewed By | Validated By |
|---|---|---|---|---|---|---|
| **Configuration Management (CM)** | | | | | | |
| **3.4.1** | **Establish and maintain baseline configurations and inventories of organizational information systems (including hardware, software, firmware, and documentation) throughout the respective system development life cycles** | | | | | |
| 3.4.1[a] | A baseline configuration is established. | | | | | |
| 3.4.1[b] | The baseline configuration includes hardware, software, firmware, and documentation. | | | | | |
| 3.4.1[c] | The baseline configuration is maintained (reviewed and updated) throughout the system development life cycle. | | | | | |
| 3.4.1[d] | A system inventory is established. | | | | | |
| 3.4.1[e] | The system inventory includes hardware, software, firmware, and documentation. | | | | | |
| 3.4.1[f] | The inventory is maintained (reviewed and updated) throughout the system development life cycle. | | | | | |
| **3.4.2** | **Establish and enforce security configuration settings for information technology products employed in organizational information systems** | | | | | |
| 3.4.2[a] | Security configuration settings for information technology products employed in the system are established and included in the baseline configuration. | | | | | |
| 3.4.2[b] | Security configuration settings for information technology products employed in the system are enforced. | | | | | |
| **3.4.3** | **Track, review, approve/disapprove, and audit changes to information systems** | | | | | |
| 3.4.3[a] | Changes to the system are tracked. | | | | | |
| 3.4.3[b] | Changes to the system are reviewed. | | | | | |

| | | |
|---|---|---|
| 3.4.3[c] | Changes to the system are approved or disapproved. | |
| 3.4.3[d] | Changes to the system are logged. | |
| **3.4.4** | **Analyze the security impact of changes prior to implementation** | |
| **3.4.5** | **Define, document, approve, and enforce physical and logical access restrictions associated with changes to the information system** | |
| 3.4.5[a] | Physical access restrictions associated with changes to the system are defined. | |
| 3.4.5[b] | Physical access restrictions associated with changes to the system are documented. | |
| 3.4.5[c] | Physical access restrictions associated with changes to the system are approved. | |
| 3.4.5[d] | Physical access restrictions associated with changes to the system are enforced. | |
| 3.4.5[e] | Logical access restrictions associated with changes to the system are defined. | |
| 3.4.5[f] | Logical access restrictions associated with changes to the system are documented. | |
| 3.4.5[g] | Logical access restrictions associated with changes to the system are approved. | |
| 3.4.5[h] | Logical access restrictions associated with changes to the system are enforced. | |
| **3.4.6** | **Employ the principle of least functionality by configuring the information system to provide only essential capabilities** | |
| 3.4.6[a] | Essential system capabilities are defined based on the principle of least functionality. | |
| 3.4.6[b] | The system is configured to provide only the defined essential capabilities. | |
| **3.4.7** | **Restrict, disable, and prevent the use of nonessential programs, functions, ports, protocols, and services** | |

| | | |
|---|---|---|
| 3.4.7[a] | Essential programs are defined. | |
| 3.4.7[b] | The use of nonessential programs is defined. | |
| 3.4.7[c] | The use of nonessential programs is restricted, disabled, or prevented as defined. | |
| 3.4.7[d] | Essential functions are defined. | |
| 3.4.7[e] | The use of nonessential functions is defined. | |
| 3.4.7[f] | The use of nonessential functions is restricted, disabled, or prevented as defined. | |
| 3.4.7[g] | Essential ports are defined. | |
| 3.4.7[h] | The use of nonessential ports is defined. | |
| 3.4.7[i] | The use of nonessential ports is restricted, disabled, or prevented as defined. | |
| 3.4.7[j] | Essential protocols are defined. | |
| 3.4.7[k] | The use of nonessential protocols is defined. | |
| 3.4.7[l] | The use of nonessential protocols is restricted, disabled, or prevented as defined. | |
| 3.4.7[m] | Essential services are defined. | |
| 3.4.7[n] | The use of nonessential services is defined. | |
| 3.4.7[o] | The use of nonessential services is restricted, disabled, or prevented as defined. | |
| 3.4.8 | Apply deny-by-exception (blacklist) policy to prevent the use of unauthorized software or deny all, permit-by-exception (whitelisting) policy to allow the execution of authorized software | |
| 3.4.8[a] | A policy specifying whether whitelisting or blacklisting is to be implemented is specified. | |
| 3.4.8[b] | The software allowed to execute under whitelisting or denied use under blacklisting is specified. | |
| 3.4.8[c] | Whitelisting to allow the execution of authorized software or blacklisting to prevent the use of unauthorized software is implemented as specified. | |
| 3.4.9 | Control and monitor user-installed software | |
| 3.4.9[a] | A policy for controlling the installation of software by users is established. | |

| | |
|---|---|
| **3.4.9[b]** | *Installation of software by users is controlled based on the established policy.* |
| **3.4.9[c]** | *Installation of software by users is monitored.* |

| Control # | Description | Assessment Method* | Document (e.g., SSP or Co. Procedure Guide) | Page # | Reviewed By | Valid ated By |
|-----------|-------------|--------------------|---------------------------------------------|--------|-------------|---------------|

## Identification & Authentication (IA)

| Control # | Description |
|-----------|-------------|
| **3.5.1** | ***Identify information system users, processes acting on behalf of users, or devices*** |
| **3.5.1[a]** | *System users are identified.* |
| **3.5.1[b]** | *Processes acting on behalf of users are identified.* |
| **3.5.1[c]** | *Devices accessing the system are identified.* |
| **3.5.2** | ***Authenticate (or verify) the identities of those users, processes, or devices, as a prerequisite to allowing access to organizational information systems*** |
| **3.5.2[a]** | *The identity of each user is authenticated or verified as a prerequisite to system access.* |
| **3.5.2[b]** | *The identity of each process acting on behalf of a user is authenticated or verified as a prerequisite to system access.* |
| **3.5.2[c]** | *The identity of each device accessing or connecting to the system is authenticated or verified as a prerequisite to system access.* |
| **3.5.3** | ***Use multifactor authentication for local and network access to privileged accounts and for network access to non-privileged accounts*** |
| **3.5.3[a]** | *Privileged accounts are identified.* |
| **3.5.3[b]** | *Multifactor authentication is implemented for local access to privileged accounts.* |
| **3.5.3[c]** | *Multifactor authentication is implemented for network access to privileged accounts.* |
| **3.5.3[d]** | *Multifactor authentication is implemented for network access to non-privileged accounts.* |

| | | |
|---|---|---|
| **3.5.4** | **Employ replay-resistant authentication mechanisms for network access to privileged and nonprivileged accounts** | |
| **3.5.5** | **Prevent reuse of identifiers for a defined period** | |
| 3.5.5[a] | A period within which identifiers cannot be reused is defined. | |
| 3.5.5[b] | Reuse of identifiers is prevented within the defined period. | |
| **3.5.6** | **Disable identifiers after a defined period of inactivity** | |
| 3.5.6[a] | A period of inactivity after which an identifier is disabled is defined. | |
| 3.5.6[b] | Identifiers are disabled after the defined period of inactivity. | |
| **3.5.7** | **Enforce a minimum password complexity and change of characters when new passwords are created** | |
| 3.5.7[a] | Password complexity requirements are defined. | |
| 3.5.7[b] | Password change of character requirements are defined. | |
| 3.5.7[c] | Minimum password complexity requirements as defined are enforced when new passwords are created. | |
| 3.5.7[d] | Minimum password change of character requirements as defined are enforced when new passwords are created. | |
| **3.5.8** | **Prohibit password reuse for a specified number of generations** | |
| 3.5.8[a] | The number of generations during which a password cannot be reused is specified. | |
| 3.5.8[b] | Reuse of passwords is prohibited during the specified number of generations. | |
| **3.5.9** | **Allow temporary password use for system logons with an immediate change to a permanent password** | |

| 3.5.10 | Store and transmit only encrypted representation of passwords | |
|---|---|---|
| 3.5.10[a] | Passwords are cryptographically protected in storage. | |
| 3.5.10[b] | Passwords are cryptographically protected in transit. | |
| 3.5.11. | Obscure feedback of authentication information | |

| Control # | Description | Assessment Method* | Document (e.g., SSP or Co. Procedure Guide) | Page # | Reviewed By | Validated By |
|---|---|---|---|---|---|---|
| **Incident Response (IR)** | | | | | | |
| **3.6.1** | **Establish an operational incident-handling capability for organizational information systems that includes adequate preparation, detection, analysis, containment, recovery, and user response activities** | | | | | |
| 3.6.1[a] | An operational incident-handling capability is established. | | | | | |
| 3.6.1[b] | The operational incident-handling capability includes preparation. | | | | | |
| 3.6.1[c] | The operational incident-handling capability includes detection. | | | | | |
| 3.6.1[d] | The operational incident-handling capability includes analysis. | | | | | |
| 3.6.1[e] | The operational incident-handling capability includes containment. | | | | | |
| 3.6.1[f] | The operational incident-handling capability includes recovery. | | | | | |
| 3.6.1[g] | The operational incident-handling capability includes user response activities. | | | | | |
| **3.6.2** | **Track, document, and report incidents to appropriate officials and/or authorities both internal and external to the organization** | | | | | |
| 3.6.2[a] | Incidents are tracked. | | | | | |
| 3.6.2[b] | Incidents are documented. | | | | | |
| 3.6.2[c] | Authorities to whom incidents are to be reported are identified. | | | | | |
| 3.6.2[d] | Organizational officials to whom incidents are to be reported are identified. | | | | | |
| 3.6.2[e] | Identified authorities are notified of incidents. | | | | | |
| 3.6.2[f] | Identified organizational officials are notified of incidents. | | | | | |
| **3.6.3** | **Test the organizational incident response capability** | | | | | |

| Control # | Description | Assessment Method* | Document (e.g., SSP or Co. Procedure Guide) | Page # | Reviewed By | Validated By |
|---|---|---|---|---|---|---|
| **Maintenance (MA)** | | | | | | |
| **3.7.1** | *Perform maintenance on organizational information systems* | | | | | |
| **3.7.2** | *Provide effective controls on the tools, techniques, mechanisms, and personnel used to conduct information system maintenance* | | | | | |
| **3.7.2[a]** | *Tools used to conduct system maintenance are controlled.* | | | | | |
| **3.7.2[b]** | *Techniques used to conduct system maintenance are controlled.* | | | | | |
| **3.7.2[c]** | *Mechanisms used to conduct system maintenance are controlled.* | | | | | |
| **3.7.2[d]** | *Personnel used to conduct system maintenance are controlled.* | | | | | |
| **3.7.3** | **Ensure equipment removed for off-site maintenance is sanitized of any CUI** | | | | | |
| **3.7.4** | *Check media containing diagnostic and test programs for malicious code before the media are used in the information system* | | | | | |
| **3.7.5** | *Require multifactor authentication to establish nonlocal maintenance sessions via external network connections and terminate such connections when nonlocal maintenance is complete* | | | | | |
| **3.7.5[a]** | *Multifactor authentication is used to establish nonlocal maintenance sessions via external network connections.* | | | | | |
| **3.7.5[b]** | *Nonlocal maintenance sessions established via external network connections are terminated when nonlocal maintenance is complete.* | | | | | |

| | |
|---|---|
| **3.7.6** | *Supervise the maintenance activities of maintenance personnel without required access authorization* |

| Control # | Description | Assessment Method* | Document (e.g., SSP or Co. Procedure Guide) | Page # | Reviewed By | Validated By |
|---|---|---|---|---|---|---|
| **Media Protection (MP)** | | | | | | |
| **3.8.1** | **Protect (i.e., physically control and securely store) information system media containing CUI, both paper and digital** | | | | | |
| 3.8.1[a] | Paper media containing CUI is physically controlled. | | | | | |
| 3.8.1[b] | Digital media containing CUI is physically controlled. | | | | | |
| 3.8.1[c] | Paper media containing CUI is securely stored. | | | | | |
| 3.8.1[d] | Digital media containing CUI is securely stored. | | | | | |
| **3.8.2** | **Limit access to CUI on information system media to authorized users** | | | | | |
| **3.8.3** | **Sanitize or destroy information system media containing CUI before disposal or release for reuse** | | | | | |
| 3.8.3[a] | System media containing CUI is sanitized or destroyed before disposal. | | | | | |
| 3.8.3[b] | System media containing CUI is sanitized before it is released for reuse. | | | | | |
| **3.8.4** | **Mark media with necessary CUI markings and distribution limitations** | | | | | |
| 3.8.4[a] | Media containing CUI is marked with applicable CUI markings. | | | | | |
| 3.8.4[b] | Media containing CUI is marked with distribution limitations. | | | | | |
| **3.8.5** | **Control access to media containing CUI and maintain accountability for media during transport outside of controlled areas** | | | | | |
| 3.8.5[a] | Access to media containing CUI is controlled. | | | | | |
| 3.8.5[b] | Accountability for media containing CUI is maintained during transport outside of controlled areas. | | | | | |

| 3.8.6 | *Implement cryptographic mechanisms to protect the confidentiality of CUI stored on digital media during transport unless otherwise protected by alternative physical safeguards* |
|---|---|
| 3.8.7 | *Control the use of removable media on information system components* |
| 3.8.8 | *Prohibit the use of portable storage devices when such devices have no identifiable owner* |
| 3.8.9 | *Protect the confidentiality of backup CUI at storage locations* |

| Control # | Description | Assessment Method* | Document (e.g., SSP or Co. Procedure Guide) | Page # | Reviewed By | Validated By |
|---|---|---|---|---|---|---|
| **Personnel Security (PS)** | | | | | | |
| **3.9.1** | **Screen individuals prior to authorizing access to information systems containing CUI** | | | | | |
| **3.9.2** | **Ensure that CUI and information systems containing CUI are protected during and after personnel actions such as terminations and transfers** | | | | | |
| 3.9.2[a] | A policy and/or process for terminating system access and any credentials coincident with personnel actions is established. | | | | | |
| 3.9.2[b] | System access and credentials are terminated consistent with personnel actions such as termination or transfer. | | | | | |
| 3.9.2[c] | The system is protected during and after personnel transfer actions. | | | | | |

| Control # | Description | Assessment Method* | Document (e.g., SSP or Co. Procedure Guide) | Page # | Reviewed By | Validated By |
|---|---|---|---|---|---|---|
| **Physical Security (PP)** | | | | | | |
| **3.10.1** | *Limit physical access to organizational information systems, equipment, and the respective operating environments to authorized individuals* | | | | | |
| 3.10.1[a] | *Authorized individuals allowed physical access are identified.* | | | | | |
| 3.10.1[b] | *Physical access to organizational systems is limited to authorized individuals.* | | | | | |
| 3.10.1[c] | *Physical access to equipment is limited to authorized individuals.* | | | | | |
| 3.10.1[d] | *Physical access to operating environments is limited to authorized individuals.* | | | | | |
| **3.10.2** | *Protect and monitor the physical facility and support infrastructure for those information systems* | | | | | |
| 3.10.2[a] | *The physical facility where organizational systems reside is protected.* | | | | | |
| 3.10.2[b] | *The support infrastructure for organizational systems is protected.* | | | | | |
| 3.10.2[c] | *The physical facility where organizational systems reside is monitored.* | | | | | |
| 3.10.2[d] | *The support infrastructure for organizational systems is monitored.* | | | | | |
| **3.10.3** | *Escort visitors and monitor visitor activity* | | | | | |
| 3.10.3[a] | *Visitors are escorted.* | | | | | |
| 3.10.3[b] | *Visitor activity is monitored.* | | | | | |
| **3.10.4** | *Maintain audit logs of physical access* | | | | | |
| **3.10.5** | *Control and manage physical access devices* | | | | | |
| 3.10.5[a] | *Physical access devices are identified.* | | | | | |
| 3.10.5[b] | *Physical access devices are controlled.* | | | | | |
| 3.10.5[c] | *Physical access devices are managed.* | | | | | |

| 3.10.6 | Enforce safeguarding measures for CUI at alternate work sites (e.g., telework sites) | |
|---|---|---|
| 3.10.6[a] | Safeguarding measures for CUI are defined for alternate work sites. | |
| 3.10.6[b] | Safeguarding measures for CUI are enforced for alternate work sites. | |

| Control # | Description | Assessment Method* | Document (e.g., SSP or Co. Procedure Guide) | Page # | Reviewed By | Validated By |
|---|---|---|---|---|---|---|
| **Risk Assessments (RA)** | | | | | | |
| **3.11.1** | ***Periodically assess the risk to organizational operations (including mission, functions, image, or reputation), organizational assets, and individuals, resulting from the operation of organizational information systems and the associated processing, storage, or transmission of CUI*** | | | | | |
| 3.11.1[a] | *The frequency to assess risk to organizational operations, organizational assets, and individuals is defined.* | | | | | |
| 3.11.1[b] | *Risk to organizational operations, organizational assets, and individuals resulting from the operation of an organizational system that processes, stores, or transmits CUI is assessed with the defined frequency.* | | | | | |
| **3.11.2** | ***Scan for vulnerabilities in the information system and applications periodically and when new vulnerabilities affecting the system are identified*** | | | | | |
| 3.11.2[a] | *The frequency to scan for vulnerabilities in organizational systems and applications is defined.* | | | | | |
| 3.11.2[b] | *Vulnerability scans are performed on organizational systems with the defined frequency.* | | | | | |
| 3.11.2[c] | *Vulnerability scans are performed on applications with the defined frequency.* | | | | | |
| 3.11.2[d] | *Vulnerability scans are performed on organizational systems when new vulnerabilities are identified.* | | | | | |
| 3.11.2[e] | *Vulnerability scans are performed on applications when new vulnerabilities are identified.* | | | | | |

| 3.11.3 | Remediate vulnerabilities in accordance with assessments of risk | |
|---|---|---|
| 3.11.3[a] | Vulnerabilities are identified. | |
| 3.11.3[b] | Vulnerabilities are remediated in accordance with risk assessments. | |

| Control # | Description | Assessment Method* | Document (e.g., SSP or Co. Procedure Guide) | Page # | Reviewed By | Validated By |
|---|---|---|---|---|---|---|
| **Security Assessments (SA)** | | | | | | |
| **3.12.1** | **Periodically assess the security controls in organizational information systems to determine if the controls are effective in their application** | | | | | |
| 3.12.1[a] | *The frequency of security control assessments is defined.* | | | | | |
| 3.12.1[b] | *Security controls are assessed with the defined frequency to determine if the controls are effective in their application.* | | | | | |
| **3.12.2** | ***Develop and implement plans of action designed to correct deficiencies and reduce or eliminate vulnerabilities in organizational information systems*** | | | | | |
| 3.12.2[a] | *Deficiencies and vulnerabilities to be addressed by the plan of action are identified.* | | | | | |
| 3.12.2[b] | *A plan of action is developed to correct identified deficiencies and reduce or eliminate identified vulnerabilities.* | | | | | |
| 3.12.2[c] | *The plan of action is implemented to correct identified deficiencies and reduce or eliminate identified vulnerabilities.* | | | | | |
| **3.12.3** | ***Monitor information system security controls on an ongoing basis to ensure the continued effectiveness of the controls*** | | | | | |
| **3.12.4** | ***Develop, document, and periodically update system security plans that describe system boundaries, system environments of operation, how security requirements are implemented, and the relationships with or connections to other systems*** | | | | | |

| | | |
|---|---|---|
| **3.12.4[a]** | *A system security plan is developed.* | |
| **3.12.4[b]** | *The system boundary is described and documented in the system security plan.* | |
| **3.12.4[c]** | *The system environment of operation is described and documented in the system security plan.* | |
| **3.12.4[d]** | *The security requirements identified and approved by the designated authority as non-applicable are identified.* | |
| **3.12.4[e]** | *The method of security requirement implementation is described and documented in the system security plan.* | |
| **3.12.4[f]** | *The relationship with or connection to other systems is described and documented in the system security plan.* | |
| **3.12.4[g]** | *The frequency to update the system security plan is defined.* | |
| **3.12.4[h]** | *System security plan is updated with the defined frequency.* | |

| Control # | Description | Assessment Method* | Document (e.g., SSP or Co. Procedure Guide) | Page # | Reviewed By | Validated By |
|---|---|---|---|---|---|---|
| **System & Communications Protection (SC)** | | | | | | |
| **3.13.1** | *Monitor, control, and protect organizational communications (i.e., information transmitted or received by organizational information systems) at the external boundaries and key internal boundaries of the information systems* | | | | | |
| 3.13.1[a] | *The external system boundary is defined.* | | | | | |
| 3.13.1[b] | *Key internal system boundaries are defined.* | | | | | |
| 3.13.1[c] | *Communications are monitored at the external system boundary.* | | | | | |
| 3.13.1[d] | *Communications are monitored at key internal boundaries.* | | | | | |
| 3.13.1[e] | *Communications are controlled at the external system boundary.* | | | | | |
| 3.13.1[f] | *Communications are controlled at key internal boundaries.* | | | | | |
| 3.13.1[g] | *Communications are protected at the external system boundary.* | | | | | |
| 3.13.1[h] | *Communications are protected at key internal boundaries.* | | | | | |
| **3.13.2** | *Employ architectural designs, software development techniques, and systems engineering principles that promote effective information security within organizational information systems* | | | | | |
| 3.13.2[a] | *Architectural designs that promote effective information security are identified.* | | | | | |
| 3.13.2[b] | *Software development techniques that promote effective information security are identified.* | | | | | |
| 3.13.2[c] | *Systems engineering principles that promote effective information security are identified.* | | | | | |

| 3.13.2[d] | Identified architectural designs that promote effective information security are employed. | |
|---|---|---|
| 3.13.2[e] | Identified software development techniques that promote effective information security are employed. | |
| 3.13.2[f] | Identified systems engineering principles that promote effective information security are employed. | |
| **3.13.3** | **Separate user functionality from information system management functionality** | |
| 3.13.3[a] | User functionality is identified. | |
| 3.13.3[b] | System management functionality is identified. | |
| 3.13.3[c] | User functionality is separated from system management functionality. | |
| **3.13.4** | **Prevent unauthorized and unintended information transfer via shared system resources** | |
| **3.13.5** | **Implement subnetworks for publicly accessible system components that are physically or logically separated from internal networks** | |
| 3.13.5[a] | Publicly accessible system components are identified. | |
| 3.13.5[b] | Subnetworks for publicly accessible system components are physically or logically separated from internal networks. | |
| **3.13.6** | **Deny network communications traffic by default and allow network communications traffic by exception (i.e., deny all, permit by exception)** | |
| 3.13.6[a] | Network communications traffic is denied by default. | |
| 3.13.6[b] | Network communications traffic is allowed by exception. | |
| **3.13.7** | **Prevent remote devices from simultaneously establishing non-remote connections with the information system and communicating via some other connection to resources in external networks** | |

| Control # | Description | Assessment Method* | Document (e.g., SSP or Co. Procedure Guide) | Page # | Reviewed By | Validated By |
|---|---|---|---|---|---|---|
| **System & Communications Protection (SC)** | | | | | | |
| **3.13.8** | *Implement cryptographic mechanisms to prevent unauthorized disclosure of CUI during transmission unless otherwise protected by alternative physical safeguards* | | | | | |
| **3.13.8[a]** | *Cryptographic mechanisms intended to prevent unauthorized disclosure of CUI are identified.* | | | | | |
| **3.13.8[b]** | *Alternative physical safeguards intended to prevent unauthorized disclosure of CUI are identified.* | | | | | |
| **3.13.8[c]** | *Either cryptographic mechanisms or alternative physical safeguards are implemented to prevent unauthorized disclosure of CUI during transmission.* | | | | | |
| **3.13.9** | *Terminate network connections associated with communications sessions at the end of the sessions or after a defined period of inactivity* | | | | | |
| **3.13.9[a]** | *A period of inactivity to terminate network connections associated with communications sessions is defined.* | | | | | |
| **3.13.9[b]** | *Network connections associated with communications sessions are terminated at the end of the sessions.* | | | | | |
| **3.13.9[c]** | *Network connections associated with communications sessions are terminated after the defined period of inactivity.* | | | | | |
| **3.13.10** | *Establish and manage cryptographic keys for cryptography employed in the information system* | | | | | |
| **3.13.10[a]** | *Cryptographic keys are established whenever cryptography is employed.* | | | | | |
| **3.13.10[b]** | *Cryptographic keys are managed whenever cryptography is employed.* | | | | | |
| **3.13.11** | *Employ FIPS-validated cryptography when used to protect the confidentiality of CUI* | | | | | |

| | | |
|---|---|---|
| **3.13.12** | ***Prohibit remote activation of collaborative computing devices and provide indication of devices in use to users present at the device*** | |
| 3.13.12[a] | *Collaborative computing devices are identified.* | |
| 3.13.12[b] | *Collaborative computing devices provide indication to users of devices in use.* | |
| 3.13.12[c] | *Remote activation of collaborative computing devices is prohibited.* | |
| **3.13.13** | ***Control and monitor the use of mobile code*** | |
| 3.13.13[a] | *Use of mobile code is controlled.* | |
| 3.13.13[b] | *Use of mobile code is monitored.* | |
| **3.13.14** | ***Control and monitor the use of Voice over Internet Protocol (VoIP) technologies*** | |
| 3.13.14[a] | *Use of Voice over Internet Protocol (VoIP) technologies is controlled.* | |
| 3.13.14[b] | *Use of Voice over Internet Protocol (VoIP) technologies is monitored.* | |
| **3.13.15** | ***Protect the authenticity of communications sessions*** | |
| **3.13.16** | ***Protect the confidentiality of CUI at rest*** | |

| Control # | Description | Assessment Method* | Document | Page # | Reviewed By | Valid ated By |
|---|---|---|---|---|---|---|
| **System & Information Integrity (SI)** | | | | | | |
| **3.14.1** | ***Identify, report, and correct information and information system flaws in a timely manner*** | | | | | |
| **3.14.1[a]** | *The time within which to identify system flaws is specified.* | | | | | |
| **3.14.1[b]** | *System flaws are identified within the specified time frame.* | | | | | |
| **3.14.1[c]** | *The time within which to report system flaws is specified.* | | | | | |
| **3.14.1[d]** | *System flaws are reported within the specified time frame.* | | | | | |
| **3.14.1[e]** | *The time within which to correct system flaws is specified.* | | | | | |
| **3.14.1[f]** | *System flaws are corrected within the specified time frame.* | | | | | |
| **3.14.2** | ***Provide protection from malicious code at appropriate locations within organizational information systems*** | | | | | |
| **3.14.2[a]** | *Designated locations for malicious code protection are identified.* | | | | | |
| **3.14.2[b]** | *Protection from malicious code at designated locations is provided.* | | | | | |
| **3.14.3** | ***Monitor information system security alerts and advisories and take appropriate actions in response*** | | | | | |
| **3.14.3[a]** | *Response actions to system security alerts and advisories are identified.* | | | | | |
| **3.14.3[b]** | *System security alerts and advisories are monitored.* | | | | | |
| **3.14.3[c]** | *Actions in response to system security alerts and advisories are taken.* | | | | | |
| **3.14.4** | ***Update malicious code protection mechanisms when new releases are available*** | | | | | |
| **3.14.5** | ***Perform periodic scans of the information system and real-time scans of files from external sources as files are*** | | | | | |

| | | |
|---|---|---|
| | *downloaded, opened, or executed* | |
| **3.14.5[a]** | *The frequency for malicious code scans is defined.* | |
| **3.14.5[b]** | *Malicious code scans are performed with the defined frequency.* | |
| **3.14.5[c]** | *Real-time malicious code scans of files from external sources as files are downloaded, opened, or executed are performed.* | |
| **3.14.6** | **Monitor the information system including inbound and outbound communications traffic, to detect attacks and indicators of potential attacks** | |
| **3.14.6[a]** | *The system is monitored to detect attacks and indicators of potential attacks.* | |
| **3.14.6[b]** | *Inbound communications traffic is monitored to detect attacks and indicators of potential attacks.* | |
| **3.14.6[c]** | *Outbound communications traffic is monitored to detect attacks and indicators of potential attacks.* | |
| **3.14.7** | **Identify unauthorized use of the information system** | |
| **3.14.7[a]** | *Authorized use of the system is defined.* | |
| **3.14.7[b]** | *Unauthorized use of the system is identified.* | |

# About the Author

Mr. Russo is the former Senior Information Security Engineer within the Department of Defense's (DOD) F-35 Joint Strike Fighter program. He has an extensive background in cybersecurity and is an expert in the Risk Management Framework (RMF) and DOD Instruction 8510 which implements RMF throughout the DOD and the federal government. He holds both a Certified Information Systems Security Professional (CISSP) certification and a CISSP in information security architecture (ISSAP). He holds a 2017 certification as a Chief Information Security Officer (CISO) from the National Defense University, Washington, DC. He retired from the US Army Reserves in 2012 as the Senior Intelligence Officer.

He is the former CISO at the Department of Education wherein 2016 he led the effort to close over 95% of the outstanding US Congressional and Inspector General cybersecurity shortfall weaknesses spanning as far back as five years.

Mr. Russo is the former Senior Cybersecurity Engineer supporting the Joint Medical Logistics Development Functional Center of the Defense Health Agency (DHA) at Fort Detrick, MD. He led a team of engineering and cybersecurity professionals protecting five major Medical Logistics systems supporting over 200 DOD Medical Treatment Facilities around the globe.

In 2011, Mr. Russo was certified by the Office of Personnel Management as a graduate of the Senior Executive Service Candidate program.

From 2009 through 2011, Mr. Russo was the Chief Technology Officer at the Small Business Administration (SBA). He led a team of over 100 IT professionals in supporting an intercontinental Enterprise IT infrastructure and security operations spanning 12-time zones; he deployed cutting-edge technologies to enhance SBA's business and information sharing operations supporting the small business community.      Mr. Russo was the first-ever Program Executive Officer (PEO)/Senior Program Manager in the Office of Intelligence & Analysis at Headquarters, Department of Homeland Security (DHS), Washington, DC. Mr. Russo was responsible for the development and deployment of secure Information and Intelligence support systems for OI&A to include software applications and systems to enhance the DHS mission. He was responsible for the program management development lifecycle during his tenure at DHS.

He holds a Master of Science from the National Defense University in Government Information Leadership with a concentration in Cybersecurity and a Bachelor of Arts in Political Science with a minor in Russian Studies from Lehigh University. He holds Level III Defense Acquisition certification in Program Management, Information Technology, and Systems Engineering. He has been a member of the DOD Acquisition Corps since 2001.

# EPILOGUE

## One Year After OPM Data Breach, What Has the Government Learned?

*"...The agency now requires employees to use **two-factor authentication** to log into their computers, meaning a password and a secure card. Employees can no longer access their Gmail ® accounts from their office computers. OPM has also implemented new tools to detect malware. ...[T]he government can see all the devices connected to its networks as well as monitor the data moving into and out of the system."*

(*SOURCE: https://www.npr.org/sections/alltechconsidered/2016/06/06/480968999/one-year-after-opm-data-breach-what-has-the-government-learned*)

Syber-Risk

## System Security Plan (SSP) Template & Workbook NIST-based

https://www.amazon.com/System-Security-Plan-Template-Workbook-ebook/dp/B07BCY41D2/ref=sr_1_1?ie=UTF8&qid=1523490730&sr=8-1&keywords=system+security+plan

This is a supplement to and is designed to provide more specific, direction and guidance on completing the core NIST 800-171 artifact, the System Security Plan (SSP). This is part of an ongoing series of support documents being developed to address the recent changes and requirements levied by the Federal Government on contractors wishing to do business with the government. The intent of these supplements is to provide immediate and valuable information so business owners and their Information Technology (IT) staff need. The changes are coming rapidly for cybersecurity contract requirements. Are you ready? We plan to be ahead of the curve with you with high-quality books that can provide immediate support to the ever-growing challenges of cyber-threats to the Government and your business.

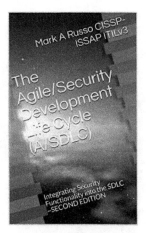

## Agile/Security Development Life Cycle (A/SDLC): Integrating Security into the System Development Life Cycle ~SECOND EDITION

(https://www.amazon.com/Agile-Security-Development-Life-Cycle-ebook/dp/B07MCRVPYX/ref=sr_1_1?keywords=agile+security+development&qid=1553130349&s=gateway&sr=8-1)

In this SECOND EDITION of THE AGILE SECURITY DEVELOPMENT LIFE CYCLE (A/SDLC) we expand and include new information to improve the concept of "Agile Cyber." We further discuss the need for a Security Traceability Requirements Matrix (SecRTM) and the need to know where all data elements are located throughout your IT environment to include Cloud storage and repository locations. The author continues his focus upon ongoing shortfalls and failures of "Secure System Development." The author seeks to use his over 25 years in the public and private sector program management and cybersecurity to create a solution. This book provides the first-ever integrated operational-security process to enhance the readers understanding of why systems are so poorly secured. Why we as a nation have missed the mark in cybersecurity? Why nation-states and hackers are successful daily? This book also describes the two major mainstream "agile" NIST frameworks that can be employed, and how to use them effectively under a Risk Management approach. We may be losing "battles, " but may be its time we truly commit to winning the cyber-war.

Syber-Risk
.com

www.ingramcontent.com/pod-product-compliance
Lightning Source LLC
Chambersburg PA
CBHW080553060326
40689CB00021B/4835